Grow Up Into Him

Bible Word Studies to Live in Victory

NEAL BERTRAND

Cypress Cove Publishing

Copyright 2018 by Neal Bertrand. All rights reserved.

Contact Neal Bertrand, author and publisher at Cypress Cove Publishing (337) 224-6576.

Or by email: neal@CypressCovePublishing.com

ISBN: 978-1-936707-50-8
Ebook ISBN: 978-1-936707-51-5
LCCN: 2018904601

Visit our websites:
CypressCovePublishing.com
DadsWarPhotos.com
RiceCookerMeals.com

Author, Editor and Publisher: Neal Bertrand
Book Design and Production: Jeremy Bertrand

Images used on book cover from Pixabay users StockSnap and Geralt

The book title is based on this scripture:
But speaking the truth in love, may GROW UP INTO HIM in all things, which is the head, even Christ.
Ephesians 4:15

Other Titles Published by Cypress Cove Publishing:
Down-Home Cajun Cooking Favorites
Rice Cooker Meals: Fast Home Cooking for Busy People
Slow Cooker Meals: Easy Home Cooking for Busy People
Cajun Country Fun Coloring and Activity Book
A House for Eliza: The Real Story of the Cajuns
Never Say Goodbye: Real Stories of the Cajuns
From Cradle to Grave: Journey of the Louisiana Orphan Train Riders
Dad's War Photos: Adventures in the South Pacific
Silent Prayer: A Spiritual Journey Toward Exposing the Occult – Level One
Trail of Six Roses: Supernatural Events at Mother's Funeral – Level Two
Mom Bradley's Crossover: From Deathbed to Heaven – Level Three
Supernatural Encounters of the Godly Kind – Level Four
Fun Times Cajun Puzzle & Activity Book

Visit CypressCovePublishing.com for all our latest books.

To order copies of this book and our other books, see our website at CypressCovePublishing.com, or call Toll Free (888) 606-3257, or buy from Barnes & Noble (BN.com) or Amazon.com

Praise For "Grow Up Into Him"

"Neal is a wonderful communicator and has a unique gift, enabling him to rightly divide God's word. In an era deprived of pure doctrine and principled teaching, Neal is able to cut through the norms of the day. You will find his writings to be life-giving!"
David Hunter - Founder of Extreme Faith International

"I just love this book! It is the perfect companion piece to the Bible! If you are a new believer, this is a wellspring of encouragement! If you love to study and read God's word, this will be a blessing to you!" Gina Hunter - Co-Pastor of Extreme Faith International

Wow ... it is hard to put this book down. It is insightful and impactful throughout its entirety. Grounded in truth and proclaimed with authority! *Grow Up Into Him* is life-changing and transforming. It should be in the possession of every true believer who wants to draw nearer and walk closer to God daily. Brilliantly written and full of wisdom.
Carrie Simon, Founder of Save Them All, Inc, Author and Child Advocate, Partner at Ardent Flame Media Group, LLC

Brother Neal Bertrand's book, *Grow Up Into Him*, is actually a handbook for those who want to grow up in Christ, breaking away from the idea that only pastors can teach you. As we desire to grow up, the Lord will also use this handbook to help others to grow up as well. No longer choking on the milk of the Word, but with real teeth to chew on the meat of the Word. - Tricia O'Connor - Welland, Ontario, Canada

Grow Up Into Him is not only for new Christians, it is also for mature Christians to be reminded of His fundamentals of the Gospel. - Tiffany King

INTRODUCTION

The Word of God is the will of God. The Word of God will always be opposite of the world's opinions and values. To grow into full Christian maturity, one must have a desire to learn the Word of God in all its fullness. By reading and meditating on God's word, we learn what His will and purpose is for all of our life. We renew our minds, strengthen our spirit, and exercise our spiritual muscles by meditating on His Word, by offering up private praise and worship, by praying, fasting and giving in secret.

Over the past 40 years I have written numerous Bible Word Studies so I could learn His Word. I did some just for fun and some I did so I could teach others at church. So, I decided to publish and print them in book form, to share my years of word study with the world.

You can see my Bible teachings and worship music on my Youtube channel. Please subscribe. www.youtube.com/user/purewordguy/playlists

That I may publish with the voice of thanksgiving, and tell of all Your wondrous works. Psalms 26:7

CONTENTS

Chapter 1: Decrees	5
Chapter 2: Scriptures to Live in Victory	8
Chapter 3: The Words of Your Mouth	11
Chapter 4: Favor with God	19
Chapter 5: The Pre-Existence of Jesus Christ	21
Chapter 6: Salvation Scriptures	24
Chapter 7: Water Baptism	35
Chapter 8: Baptism in the Holy Spirit	38
Chapter 9: Titles and Names of Jesus Christ	44
Chapter 10: What God Says about Love	51
Chapter 11: The Kingdom in Revelation and Daniel	55
Chapter 12: Overcoming Fear	58
Chapter 13: Our Heavenly Father	60
Chapter 14: Divine Guidance	71
Chapter 15: Your Thinking, Thoughts, and Imaginations	73
Chapter 16: Faith Scriptures	74
Chapter 17: Prosperity Scriptures	76
Chapter 18: The Occult, Psychics, and Witchcraft	86
Chapter 19: Jesus Rose From The Dead	90
Chapter 20: The Light of the Body is the Eye	96
Chapter 21: How to Overcome Lust	100
Chapter 22: I have Power over Sin and Addiction	104
Chapter 23: Romans Chapter Six	105
Chapter 24: How to Stop Sinning	106
Chapter 25: Transfiguration of Jesus	107
Chapter 26: Jesus Paid For your Healing on the Cross	109
Chapter 27: Healing of Feet	112
Chapter 28: Healing the Wounded Spirit	113
Chapter 29: Restoring the Carnal Mind	115
Chapter 30: Stable in all Your Ways	118
Chapter 31: Scriptures Concerning Your Children	119
Chapter 32: Deliverance Authority	120
Chapter 33: How to Pray for the Lost	126
Chapter 34: Preaching the Gospel	128
Chapter 35: Seeking God	135
About the Author	139

CHAPTER 1

DECREES

Below is what Pastor Elvin Norsworthy of Celebration Church in Baton Rouge and Lafayette, Louisiana has us repeat after him before he starts preaching his message.

PASTOR ELVIN DECREES:

Grab your Bible and say out loud:
"This is my Bible. It is the word of God. I am what it says I am. I have what it says I have. I can do what it says I can do. God is who he says he is. God has what he says he has. God will do what he says he can do. This is my season. This is my year. This is my year that my dreams come true. To God be all the glory for the great things he has done. In blessing, he blesses me. In multiplying He multiplies me. Everything I set my hands to, absolutely everything, always prospers, it must prosper, it will prosper every time, all the time. I am full of Jesus, I am full of the Holy Ghost. I am highly favored. I am highly anointed."

DECREES FOR PROVISION
By Clarice Fluitt
Please visit her site: https://claricefluitt.org/

Without faith it is impossible to please God. (Hebrews 11:6) These words must come out of your heart and out of your mouth and they will become yours by reason of use. This is putting your faith in God and speaking words until they become a reality to you. Decree these OUT LOUD upon arising every morning and every night before bedtime.

I, __(say your name)__ , declare that I have a vision for divine provision. I am an end time financier. I'm a marketplace minister, and as such, I have the privilege and biblical responsibility to tithe, to give offerings, and to support the kingdom of God as a marketplace minister.

I know the calling includes and goes beyond the boundaries of the local church. As a marketplace minister, I will enlarge my vision and I will concentrate on influencing and transforming key components of society. This includes education, media, entertainment, government, transforming the arts to bring an understanding of the revelation of God.

Because I love God's Word, I am a candidate to increase in wisdom and in wealth. I choose to guard my heart with all diligence. (Proverbs 4:23) I decree that poverty is a curse and it cannot come near my dwelling.

The word of God in 3 John 2 teaches that above all things God desires that I prosper and be in health as my soul prospers. I have learned to speak to my body and I'm telling my body, my soul and my spirit to get in line with the word of God. I decree wholeness into my life. I refuse sickness in my life.

I decree money is an important tool, a tool that will enable me to accomplish great and mighty things that God has called and created me to do. Money magnifies what's in my heart and what is in my heart is God, and money is the course that I need to enforce and activate the will of God.

Money is to serve the call of God according to Matthew 6:24. (No man can serve two masters: for either he will hate the one and love the other; or else he will hold to the one and despise the other. Ye cannot serve God and mammon.)

Money is a tool for global harvest according to Philippians 4:15-17. Money will expose a spirit of poverty according to Deuteronomy 8:18 - God gives me the power to get wealth. (Deuteronomy 8:18 But thou shalt remember the LORD thy God: for it is he that giveth thee power to get wealth, that he may establish his covenant which he sware unto thy fathers, as it is this day.)

I am a person of breakthrough according to Micah 2:13. (One who breaks open the way will advance before them; they will break out, pass through the city gate, and leave by it. Their King will pass through before them, the LORD as their leader. (Christian Standard Bible)

I am a divine radical for God. I pursue the purpose of God for supernatural favor and financial breakthrough. I've been created to support and promote the cause of Christ. I am a forceful, faithful person. I am called. I am equipped. I am investing into missions and I will send the gospel around the world. I am generous to the poor and needy. My God takes delight in my prosperity. He is El Shaddai. I decree my God is more than enough.

I declare now that I have broken through into the dimensions of multiplication. I decree I have the spirit of generosity and mammon does not have any hold upon me.
I decree that I have supernatural favor with God and man, and things cannot have me. I will have those things that God has said so I can be generous and provide for others. I decree that giving to God opens the gate of unlimited favor that will flow into my life.

DECREE OF 1 CORINTHIANS 1:4-9 by Gale Despino McGlothlin

I believe God made you the way He wants you. He is not taken by surprise. Ever! Do this spiritual exercise.
Lay down your thought processes briefly each day, look in the mirror and quote 1 Corinthians 1:4-9, hearing the Word with your heart of love for Father and Jesus, knowing He is <u>for</u> you, never <u>against</u> you. And I ask that you do this at least three times a day; but 10 times a day would be awesome. It's a simple exercise wherein you do not think on others' success, or your problems. It gives your mind a break and the Pure Word will begin to make your heart of hearts jump with excitement. Allow that to flow.
Use your imagination to see Jesus confirming you to His Father and the Father inviting you into fellowship with His dear Son. Use your imagination and make the events grandiose, like a huge fancy throne room with elegant steps up to the throne where He is high and lifted up, where YOU are the invited guest to go up. Will you do that?

The scriptures below are in four versions. Pick the version you like the best and read that one… or read all four to get a more complete understanding of what God is speaking to you. **You should make it personal** as if you are claiming these promises for yourself.

You can write your favorite version on an index card and tape it to your bathroom mirror. These versions can be found at www.biblegateway.com.

1 Corinthians 1:4-9

4 I thank my God always concerning you for the grace of God which was given to you by Christ Jesus, 5 that you were enriched in everything by Him in all utterance and all knowledge, 6 even as the testimony of Christ was confirmed in you, 7 so that you come short in no gift, eagerly waiting for the revelation of our Lord Jesus Christ, 8 who will also confirm you to the end, that you may be blameless in the day of our Lord Jesus Christ. 9 God is faithful, by whom you were called into the fellowship of His Son, Jesus Christ our Lord. **(New King James Version)**

4 I thank my God always for you because of the grace of God which was given you in Christ Jesus, 5 so that in everything you were [exceedingly] enriched in Him, in all speech [empowered by the spiritual gifts] and in all knowledge [with insight into the faith]. 6 In this way our testimony about Christ was confirmed and established in you, 7 so that you are not lacking in any spiritual gift [which comes from the Holy Spirit], as you eagerly wait [with confident trust] for the revelation of our Lord Jesus Christ [when He returns]. 8 And He will also confirm you to the end [keeping you strong and free of any accusation, so that you will be] blameless and beyond reproach in the day [of the return] of our Lord Jesus Christ. 9 God is faithful [He is reliable, trustworthy and ever true to His promise—He can be depended on], and through Him you were called into fellowship with His Son, Jesus Christ our Lord. **(Amplified Bible)**

4 I always thank my God for you because of the ·grace [gift; favor] God has given you in Christ Jesus. 5 I thank God because in Christ you have been ·made rich [enriched] in every way, in all your ·speaking [or spiritual gifts of speaking] and in all your ·knowledge [or gifts of spiritual knowledge]. 6 Just as our ·witness [testimony; message] about Christ has been ·guaranteed to [or confirmed among] you, 7 so you ·have every [L do not lack any] ·gift from God [spiritual gift; L gift] while you wait for the ·return [L revelation] of our Lord Jesus Christ. 8 ·Jesus [L …who] will keep you strong until the end so that ·there will be no wrong in you [you will be blameless/faultless] on the day ·our Lord Jesus Christ comes again [L of our Lord Jesus Christ; C the final day of judgment, known in the OT as "the Day of the Lord"]. 9 God, who has called you into ·fellowship [partnership; relationship] with his Son, Jesus Christ our Lord, is faithful. **(Expanded Bible)**

4 I give thanks to my God always concerning you for the grace of God that was given to you in Christ Jesus, 5 that in every thing ye were enriched in him, in all discourse and all knowledge,6 according as the testimony of the Christ was confirmed in you,7 so that ye are not behind in any gift, waiting for the revelation of our Lord Jesus Christ,8 who also shall confirm you unto the end – unblameable in the day of our Lord Jesus Christ;9 faithful [is] God, through whom ye were called to the fellowship of His Son Jesus Christ our Lord. **(Young's Literal Translation)**

Prayer for Givers

<u>Personalize this Prayer to make it real for you:</u>

In Jesus name I proclaim blessing over these people of God in their giving as they fund the work of the kingdom in this house, in every ministry that we impact, in this country and internationally.

I proclaim the blessing of God and his abundance over you and break the power of a poverty spirit.

I break the power of fear of lack, and I break the power of a religious spirit that thinks having less makes you more holy.

I declare the sonship adoption of God over each and every person here today and the financial provision and blessing that comes with being a co-heir with Jesus Christ whose blood makes us sinless and spotless, in whom we have all of our provision in all of our inheritance.

And Lord I ask that you multiply the financial blessing of these people and that their hearts will be open to receive it with gratitude, with wisdom, and with faithfulness, and in turn be just as generous as you, God, have been generous to us. That your name Jesus may be made famous in all the earth. In Jesus' name I pray. Amen

by Gannon Lamson, Executive Pastor, Vineyard Church of Lafayette, La.

CHAPTER 2

CONFESS THESE SCRIPTURES OUT LOUD TO LIVE IN VICTORY

When I became a new Christian, I read these scriptures every morning. By doing this, it kept the Word of God fresh in my heart. Eventually I had memorized all of them. Personalize them to make the Word real to you.

Hebrews 11.1 Now faith is the substance of things hoped for, the evidence of things not seen.

Hebrews 11.6 But without faith [it is] impossible to please [him]: for he that cometh to God must believe that he is, and [that] he is a rewarder of them that diligently seek him.

Psalm 91:1-16 He that dwelleth in the secret place of the most High shall abide under the shadow of the Almighty.

2 I will say of the LORD, [He is] my refuge and my fortress: my God; in him will I trust.

3 Surely he shall deliver thee from the snare of the fowler, [and] from the noisome pestilence.

4 He shall cover thee with his feathers, and under his wings shalt thou trust: his truth [shall be thy] shield and buckler.

5 Thou shalt not be afraid for the terror by night; [nor] for the arrow [that] flieth by day;

6 [Nor] for the pestilence [that] walketh in darkness; [nor] for the destruction [that] wasteth at noonday.

7 A thousand shall fall at thy side, and ten thousand at thy right hand; [but] it shall not come nigh thee.

8 Only with thine eyes shalt thou behold and see the reward of the wicked.
9 Because thou hast made the LORD, [which is] my refuge, [even] the most High, thy habitation;
10 There shall no evil befall thee, neither shall any plague come nigh thy dwelling.
11 For he shall give his angels charge over thee, to keep thee in all thy ways.
12 They shall bear thee up in [their] hands, lest thou dash thy foot against a stone.
13 Thou shalt tread upon the lion and adder: the young lion and the dragon shalt thou trample under feet.
14 Because he hath set his love upon me, therefore will I deliver him: I will set him on high, because he hath known my name.
15 He shall call upon me, and I will answer him: I [will be] with him in trouble; I will deliver him, and honour him.
16 With long life will I satisfy him, and shew him my salvation.

Mark 11.23 For verily I say unto you, That whosoever shall say unto this mountain, Be thou removed, and be thou cast into the sea; and shall not doubt in his heart, but shall believe that those things which he saith shall come to pass; he shall have whatsoever he saith.
Mark 11.24 Therefore I say unto you, What things soever ye desire, when ye pray, believe that ye receive [them], and ye shall have [them].

Matthew 6.33 But seek ye first the kingdom of God, and his righteousness; and all these things shall be added unto you.
Matthew 6.34 Take therefore no thought for the morrow: for the morrow shall take thought for the things of itself. Sufficient unto the day [is] the evil thereof.

Mark 9.23 Jesus said unto him, If thou canst believe, all things [are] possible to him that believeth.

Nehemiah 8.10 ... for the joy of the LORD is your strength.

1 John 4.4 Ye are of God, little children, and have overcome them: because greater is he that is in you, than he that is in the world.

Ephesians 1.21 Far above all principality, and power, and might, and dominion, and every name that is named, not only in this world, but also in that which is to come:

Ephesians 2.6 And hath raised [us] up together, and made [us] sit together in heavenly [places] in Christ Jesus:

Isaiah 53.4 Surely he hath borne our griefs, and carried our sorrows: yet we did esteem him stricken, smitten of God, and afflicted.
Isaiah 53.5 But he [was] wounded for our transgressions, [he was] bruised for our iniquities: the chastisement of our peace [was] upon him; and with his stripes we are healed.

Philippians 4.4 Rejoice in the Lord always: [and] again I say, Rejoice.

Philippians 4.8 Finally, brethren, whatsoever things are true, whatsoever things [are] honest, whatsoever things [are] just, whatsoever things [are] pure, whatsoever things [are] lovely, whatsoever things [are] of good report; if [there be] any virtue, and if [there be] any praise, think on these things.

Philippians 4.13 I can do all things through Christ which strengtheneth me.

Philippians 4.19 But my God shall supply all your need according to his riches in glory by Christ Jesus.

Psalms 84.11 For the LORD God [is] a sun and shield: the LORD will give grace and glory: no good [thing] will he withhold from them that walk uprightly.

Psalms 34.9 O fear the LORD, ye his saints: for [there is] no want to them that fear him.

Psalms 34.10 The young lions do lack, and suffer hunger: but they that seek the LORD shall not want any good [thing].

Psalms 68.19 Blessed [be] the Lord, [who] daily loadeth us [with benefits, even] the God of our salvation. Selah.

2 Timothy 1.7 For God hath not given us the spirit of fear; but of power, and of love, and of a sound mind.

Romans 8.37 Nay, in all these things we are more than conquerors through him that loved us.

Psalms 25.4 Shew me thy ways, O LORD; teach me thy paths.

Psalms 25.5 Lead me in thy truth, and teach me: for thou [art] the God of my salvation; on thee do I wait all the day.

Romans 8.32 He that spared not his own Son, but delivered him up for us all, how shall he not with him also freely give us all things?

Psalms 37.23 The steps of a [good] man are ordered by the LORD: and he delighteth in his way.

Psalms 27.1 The LORD [is] my light and my salvation; whom shall I fear? the LORD [is] the strength of my life; of whom shall I be afraid?

Psalms 118.24 This [is] the day [which] the LORD hath made; we will rejoice and be glad in it.

Micah 3.8 But truly I am full of power by the spirit of the LORD, and of judgment, and of might, to declare unto Jacob his transgression, and to Israel his sin.

2 Corinthians 2.14 Now thanks [be] unto God, which always causeth us to triumph in Christ, and maketh manifest the savour of his knowledge by us in every place.

Luke 10.19 Behold, I give unto you power to tread on serpents and scorpions, and over all the power of the enemy: and nothing shall by any means hurt you.

The Prayers of Paul in Ephesians Chapters One and Three

Ephesians 1.17-19 That the God of our Lord Jesus Christ, the Father of glory, may give unto you the spirit of wisdom and revelation in the knowledge of him:
1.18 The eyes of your understanding being enlightened; that ye may know what is the hope of his calling, and what the riches of the glory of his inheritance in the saints,
1.19 And what [is] the exceeding greatness of his power to us-ward who believe, according to the working of his mighty power,

Ephesians 3.16-21 That he would grant you, according to the riches of his glory, to be strengthened with might by his Spirit in the inner man;
17 That Christ may dwell in your hearts by faith; that ye, being rooted and grounded in love,
18 May be able to comprehend with all saints what [is] the breadth, and length, and depth, and height;
19 And to know the love of Christ, which passeth knowledge, that ye might be filled with all the fulness of God.
20 Now unto him that is able to do exceeding abundantly above all that we ask or think, according to the power that worketh in us,
21 Unto him [be] glory in the church by Christ Jesus throughout all ages, world without end. Amen.

CHAPTER 3

THE WORDS OF YOUR MOUTH

We must learn to control our tongue and use it for blessing and not for evil. These scriptures reveal what God's attitude is concerning our words we speak.

Psalms 141:3 Set a guard, O Lord, before my mouth; keep watch at the door of my lips.
(God's angels are watching the words of my mouth.)

Psalms 19:14 Let the words of my mouth, and the meditation of my heart, be acceptable in Thy sight, O Lord, my strength, and my Redeemer.
(I only allow the words of my mouth, and the meditation of my heart, to be those that are acceptable in Thy sight.)

Psalms 17:3 I am purposed that my mouth shall not transgress.
(My thoughts pass not over my mouth.) Young's Literal Translation (YLT)

Psalms 39:1 I said, I will take heed to my ways, that I sin not with my tongue: I will keep my mouth with a bridle, while the wicked is before me.
YLT I have said, 'I observe my ways against sinning with my tongue, I keep for my mouth a curb, while the wicked is before me.'

Psalms 50:23 Whoso offereth praise glorifieth me: and to him that ordereth his conversation (his conduct, way, behavior) aright will I show the salvation of God.

Matthew 12:34 Out of the abundance (overflow) of the heart the mouth speaks.
For whatever is in your heart determines what you say. **New Living Translation (NLT)**
Matthew 12:35 A good man out of the good treasure of the heart brings (flings) forth good things: and an evil man out of the evil treasure brings forth evil things.
Matthew 12:36 But I say unto you, that every **idle** (inoperative, non-working) word that men shall speak, they shall give account thereof in the day of judgment. (**Idle** = free from labor, at leisure; lazy, shunning the labour which one ought to perform) (NLT- you must give an account on judgment day for every idle word you speak.
Matthew 12:37 For by thy words thou shalt be **justified**, (to show one to be righteous) and by thy words thou shalt be condemned. (NLT- The words you say will either acquit you or condemn you.)

(My heart overflows with an abundance of God's word and Holy Spirit. My words are full of energetic life-giving words that create God's divine power, restoration and healing. I fling out Divine healing and restoration from my spirit.)

Jesus told parables with no idle words. The parable of the good Samaritan was told in 204 words in 8 verses. Jesus made very efficient use of his words.

Matthew 5:34 But I say unto you, **Swear** not at all (do not bind yourself by an **oath**; to affirm, promise, threaten, with an oath), neither by heaven, for it is God's throne: (oath = a fence; a limit, i.e. sacred restraint)
Matthew 5:35 Nor by the earth, for it is His footstool; neither by Jerusalem, for it is the city of the great King.
Matthew 5:36 Neither shalt thou swear by thy head, because thou canst not make one hair white or black.
Matthew 5:37 But let your communication be "yea, yea; nay, nay;" for whatsoever is more than these cometh of evil (comes from the evil one). **D + evil = devil. I only speak "yes and no." I do not permit devil words to exit my mouth.**

Ephesians 4:29 Let no **corrupt** communication proceed out of your mouth, but only that which is good to the use of **edifying**, that it may minister grace unto the hearers. (NLT- Don't use foul or abusive language. Let everything you say be good and helpful, so that your words will be an encouragement to those who hear them.)
Corrupt - rotten, putrefied; no longer fit for use, worn out; of poor quality, bad, unfit for use, worthless
Edifying = from edifice, a building; To instruct, especially so as to encourage intellectual, moral, or spiritual improvement. Jude 20 = praying in the spirit edifies, builds you up

Ephesians 4:29 (Amplified) Let no foul or polluting language, nor evil word, nor unwholesome or worthless talk ever come out of your mouth; but only such speech as is good and beneficial to the spiritual progress of others, as is fitting to the need and the occasion, that it may be a blessing and give grace (God's favor) to those who hear it.

(I only speak what is good and beneficial to the spiritual progress of others, as is fitting to the need and the occasion, that it may be a blessing and give grace (God's favor) to those who hear it.)

Ephesians 5:4 Neither filthiness, nor foolish talking, nor jesting, which are not convenient: but rather giving of thanks. (NLT - Obscene stories, foolish talk, and coarse jokes—these are not for you. Instead, let there be thankfulness to God.)

Ephesians 5:4 (Amp) Let there be no filthiness (obscenity, indecency, shamefulness) nor **foolish**(morologia = moronic, silly talk) and sinful, corrupt talk, nor coarse jesting, which are not fitting or becoming; but instead voice your thankfulness to God.

foolish talking = silly, idle talk; randomness of conversation; lack of forethought and wisdom; useless talk; folly; no taking account of words; a sign of nearsightedness and unlearned as to the value and significance of words; ridicule. Every word you speak is used!

jesting = pleasantry, humor, facetiousness; easily turning, nimble-witted, witty, sharp, that which turns easily; has a sense of versatility; easily turns and adapts to moods and conditions of those you are dealing with; polished and witty speech used as an instrument of sin to cut down others; without flavor of Christian grace; a sly question; a smart answer; tart irony; mockery, shrewd imitation; bold scheme of speech; acute nonsense; hidden in language; sarcasm. The Greek word for sarcasm means "flesh-tearing." You are tearing up someone with your witty barbs. ("The little foxes spoil the vine.")

facetious = Playfully jocular; humorous
1. characterized by levity of attitude and love of joking: a facetious person.
2. jocular or amusing, esp at inappropriate times:
3. not meant to be taken seriously or literally: a facetious remark.
4. lacking serious intent:
cleverly amusing in tone; "a bantering tone;" "facetious remarks;" "tongue-in-cheek advice"

Colossians 4:6 Let your speech be always with grace, seasoned with salt, that you may know how you ought to answer every man. (NLT Let your conversation be gracious and attractive so that you will have the right response for everyone.)

grace = that which affords joy, pleasure, delight, sweetness, charm, loveliness: grace of speech; good will, loving-kindness, favor

seasoned = full of wisdom and grace, pleasant and wholesome

salt = salt is a symbol of lasting concord

Matthew 15:11 ...that which comes out of the mouth defiles a man. (NLT- It's not what goes into your mouth that defiles you; you are defiled by the words that come out of your mouth.)

"Make sure brain is engaged before putting mouth in gear."
I only permit blessing and life to flow from my mouth.

James 1:19 Wherefore, my beloved brethren, let every man be swift to hear, slow to speak, slow to wrath.

(I am swift to hear, I am slow to speak, I am slow to wrath. I am controlling my tongue.)

James 1:26 If any man among you seem to be religious, and he bridles (controls) not his tongue, but deceives his own heart (inner man), this man's religion is vain.(NLT- If you claim to be religious but don't control your tongue, you are fooling yourself, and your religion is worthless.)

(I control my tongue, my spirit and heart are purified, sanctified and I decree divine life to all.)

James 3:2 For in many things we offend all. If any man offend not in word, the same is a perfect man (a mature, fully developed character), and able also to bridle (control) the whole body (and curb his entire nature). (NLT- Indeed, we all make many mistakes. For if we could control our tongues, we would be perfect and could also control ourselves in every other way.)

(I am a perfect man, wonderfully made by God. I am a mature, fully developed character, with a fully awakened spirit. Every part of my spirit anatomy is fully functioning the way God designed me to be. I bridle and control my perfectly whole body and soul.)

James 3:3 Behold, we put bits in horse's mouths that they may obey us; and we turn about their whole body.

James 3:4 Behold also the ships, which though they be so great, and are driven of fierce winds, yet are they turned about with a very small helm (rudder), whithersoever the governor (captain) determines.

James 3:5 Even so the tongue is a little member, and boasts great things. Behold how great a matter a little fire kindles! (the tongue is kindling).

James 3:6 And the tongue is a fire, a world of iniquity: so is the tongue among our members, that it defiles the whole body, and sets on fire the course of nature; and it is set on fire of hell. (Consider this: so is the tongue among our members of the Body of Christ, that it defiles (is contagious to) the whole body of believers. Have you ever noticed how foolish talking is contagious?)

James 3:7 For every kind of beasts, and of birds, and of serpents, and of things in the sea, is tamed, and has been tamed of mankind:

James 3:8 But the tongue can no man <u>tame</u>; (Tame = to restrain, to curb); it is an unruly (undisciplined, restless) evil, full of deadly poison. [However... Proverbs 16:23 – The heart of the wise (full of the Holy Spirit and the Word) teaches his mouth, and adds learning to his lips.]

James 3:9 Therewith we bless God, even the Father; and therewith we curse men, which are made after the similitude of God. (NLT- Sometimes it praises our Lord and Father, and sometimes it curses those who have been made in the image of God.)

James 3:10 Out of the same mouth proceeds blessing and cursing. My brethren, these things ought not to be so.

James 3:11 Does a fountain send forth at the same place sweet water and bitter?

James 3:12...so can no fountain both yield salt water and fresh.

(My heart is wise and overflowing with the Holy Spirit and the Word. God is teaching me and I am learning.)

James 4:11 Speak not evil one of another, brethren. He that speaks evil of his brother, and judges his brother, speaks evil of the law, and judges the law: but if you judge the law, you are not a doer of the law, but a judge.

James 5:9 Grudge not one against another brethren, lest you be condemned: behold, the judge stands before the door. (NLT- Don't grumble about each other, brothers and sisters, or you will be judged. For look—the Judge is standing at the door!)
The grudge judge is judging your grudges.
Amp version. Do not complain, brethren, against one another, so that you yourselves may not be judged.

James 5:12 But above all things, my brethren, swear not, neither by heaven, neither by the earth, neither by any other oath: but let your yea be yea; and your nay, nay; lest you fall into (under) condemnation.

Proverbs 8:13 The fear of the Lord is to hate...the froward mouth. Froward = obstinate; stubbornly contrary, disobedient; not easily managed. Habitually disposed to disobedience and opposition.
Given to acting in opposition to others:
(YLT) The fear of Jehovah is to hate evil; Pride, and arrogance, and an evil way, And a froward mouth, I have hated.
(NLT All who fear the LORD will hate evil. Therefore, I hate pride and arrogance, corruption and perverse speech.)

Proverbs 4:23 Keep thy heart with all diligence; for out of it are the issues of life. (Issues = source of life.)
(NLT Guard your heart above all else, for it determines the course of your life.)
(I protect and guard my heart diligently so the flow of the Spirit comes out of me as a river of Divine LIFE!)

Proverbs 4:24 Put away from thee a froward (disobedient, contrary) mouth, and perverse lips put far from thee.
Perverse = Contrary to what is right, good, expected, or reasonable; wicked or depraved:
(NLT Avoid all perverse talk; stay away from corrupt speech.)

Proverbs 6:2 Thou art snared with the words of thy mouth, thou art taken (captive) with the words of your mouth. **(Snared by good words as well as bad.)**
(NLT- if you have trapped yourself by your agreement and are caught by what you said—)
(YLT- (if thou) Hast been snared with sayings of thy mouth, Hast been captured with sayings of thy mouth,)
(I speak forth and decree powerful divine life-filled words of healing and restoration to myself and others. I am snared, taken captive and surrounded by Divine Life, blessings and restoration. My spirit is fully awakened and operating in all the Gifts and fruit of the Holy Spirit. I am operating in the gift of discerning of spirits. I have entered into the Kingdom of God, I see God's Kingdom clearly.)

Proverbs 6:16 These six things does the Lord hate: yea, seven are an **abomination** unto Him:
(NLT seven things he detests)
Abomination = that which is exceptionally loathsome, hateful, sinful, wicked, or vile.
Proverbs 6:17 A proud look, (NLT haughty eyes,) a lying tongue, and hands that shed innocent blood,
Proverbs 6:18 A heart that devises wicked imaginations, feet that be swift in running to mischief,
Proverbs 6:19 A false witness that speaks lies, and he that soweth **discord** among brethren (gossip).
(NOTE: 3 out of 7 things God hates deals with the tongue)
Discord = Lack of agreement among persons, groups, or things; conflict.

Proverbs 10:11 The mouth of a righteous man is a well of life.
(My mouth is a well of divine life, and I decree blessing, wisdom and restoration.)

Proverbs 10:13 In the lips of him that has understanding wisdom is found.
(NLT Wise words come from the lips of people with understanding)

Proverbs 10:19 In the multitude of words there wanteth (lacks) not sin: but he that refrains his lips is wise.
(NLT Too much talk leads to sin. Be sensible and keep your mouth shut.)
(Some people talk so much it seems they have a Bionic Mouth.)

Proverbs 11:12 A man of understanding holds his peace

Proverbs 12:18 There is he that speaks like the piercings of a sword: but the tongue of the wise is health (brings healing).
(I speak and decree Divine health, Divine healing, Divine life and Divine restoration.)

Proverbs 14:23 In all labor there is profit: but the (idle) talk of the lips tends only to poverty.

Proverbs 15:4 A wholesome tongue is a tree of life: but perverseness (willful contrariness) therein is a breach (breaking, fracture, crushing, shattering) in the spirit (your inner man).

Proverbs 18:6 A fool's lips enter into contention (strife, controversy, dispute), and his mouth invites a beating.
Proverbs 18:7 A fool's mouth is his destruction, and his lips are the snare of his soul.

Proverbs 18:8 & Proverbs 26:22 The words of a talebearer (to whisper, murmur, backbite, slander) are as wounds (tender morsels gulped down by gossip gluttons starving for gossip), and they go down into the innermost parts of the belly (spirit man).

(The words of a righteous man filled with God's word and Spirit bring Divine Healing, Life, Blessings, and Restoration.)

Proverbs 18:21 Death and life are in the power of the tongue: and they that love it shall eat the fruit thereof.
(Divine LIFE and Anointing is in the power of my tongue. I am speaking forth the redeeming power of the resurrected Christ. I am imparting God's healing! Sickness and disease must depart from the presence of God in me. I am speaking forth Divine encouragement and Hope! Miracles are always happening in my presence.)

Proverbs 21:23 Whoso keeps his mouth and his tongue keeps his soul from troubles.

Ecclesiastes 5:1-7 Keep thy foot when thou goest to the house of God, and be more ready to hear, than to give the sacrifice of fools: for they consider not that they do evil.
2 Be not rash with thy mouth, and let not thine heart be hasty to utter any thing before God: for God is in heaven, and thou upon earth: therefore let thy words be few.
3 For a dream cometh through a multitude of business (work, travail); and a fool's voice is known by multitude of words.
4 When thou vowest a vow unto God, defer not to pay it; for he hath no pleasure in fools: pay that which thou hast vowed.
5 Better is it that thou shouldst not vow, than that thou shouldst vow and not pay.
6 Suffer not (permit not) thy mouth to cause thy flesh to sin; neither say thou before the angel, that "it was an error." ("I didn't mean it"): wherefore should God be angry at thy voice, and destroy the work of thine hands?
7 For in the multitude of many words there are divers (various) vanities: but fear thou God. (but as for you, fear God.)
(I pay my vows, I live a holy life, I speak right, truth-filled words; therefore, God will not be angry at the sound of my voice and He will not destroy the works of my hands. But rather, my words bring blessings.)

2 Timothy 2:21 If a man therefore purge himself from **these**, he shall be a vessel unto honor, sanctified, and meet (fit) for the Master's use, and prepared unto every good work. What are "these?":
2 Timothy 2:14 ...striving about words to no profit, which subvert the hearers.
2 Timothy 2:16 profane and vain babblings which is ungodliness
2 Timothy 2:17 evil words which eat as does a cancer and that subvert and cause doubt.
2 Timothy 2:18 lies, false teaching
2 Timothy 2:22 youthful lusts
2 Timothy 2:23 foolish and unlearned questions which gender strife
(Get rid of these evil behaviors listed above of bad words and actions in order that "you may recover yourself out of the snare of the devil, who (you) are taken captive (Proverbs 6:2) by him (devil) at his will."

Psalms 119:11 Thy Word have I hid in my heart that I might not sin against thee.

The Positive Aspect Of Your Words

Isaiah 50:4 The Lord God has given me the tongue of the learned, that I should know how to speak a word in season to him that is weary: He wakens me morning by morning, He wakens my ear to hear as the learned.

Isaiah 50:5 The Lord God has opened my ear, and I was not rebellious, neither turned away back.

(Just as you are about to wake up, listen for God to speak to you.)

John 6:63 It is the spirit that quickens (gives life); the flesh profits nothing: the words that I speak unto you, they are spirit, and they are life.

1 Peter 4:11 If any man speak, let him speak as the oracles (utterances) of God; if any man minister, let him do it as of the ability which God gives: that God in all things may be glorified through Jesus Christ, to Whom be praise and dominion for ever and ever. Amen.

Mark 11:22 Jesus said, Have the faith of God. Verse 23 tells you how:

Mark 11:23 Verily, verily I say unto you, that whosoever shall say unto this mountain (this problem), Be thou removed and be thou cast into the sea (faith command), and shall not doubt in his heart (that those things which he saith shall come to pass), but shall believe (in his heart) that those things which he saith shall come to pass, he shall have whatsoever he saith!

The practical illustration of the God kind of faith is given us in Genesis Chapter 1. God SAID, "Let there be light" and "God saw." The God kind of faith says it and sees it.

1 Samuel 3:19 And Samuel grew, and the Lord was with him, and did let none of his <u>words fall to the ground.</u>

Mark 11:23 ...but shall believe that those things which he saith shall come to pass...

Do not say anything that you do not want to come to pass. We should be able to believe that whatever we say will come to pass; no idle words, no words void of power and truth, so God won't let any of your words fall to the ground.

I am operating in Jesus' blood Covenant, therefore my faith-filled words always manifest.

Job 22:28 Thou shalt also **decree** a thing, and it shall be established unto thee: and the light shall shine upon thy ways.

<u>Decree</u> = To decide permanently where it cannot be altered.

SAY THIS:

I decree using my faith-filled words. What I decree always manifests!

Psalms 107:20 He sent His WORD and healed them and delivered them from their destructions.

John 3:34 For since He whom God has sent speaks (only) the words of God - proclaims God's own message - God does not give Him His Spirit sparingly or by measure, but boundless is the gift God makes of His Spirit.

(I am sent by God to this earth to bless people. I speak God's word. I am in Christ. I am one with Christ. I am a joint heir with Christ. God's Spirit in me flows freely and abundantly to others! God's anointing in me is without measure. God's gifts of His Holy Spirit are flowing exceedingly abundantly in me.)

1 Timothy 4:12 ...be thou an example of the believers in speech and in your behavior...

Matthew 9:6 But that you may know that the Son of man has power on earth to forgive sins, (then saith he to the sick of the palsy), Arise, take up thy bed, and go unto thine house.
Matthew 9:7 And he arose, and departed to his house.
Matthew 9:8 But when the multitudes saw it, they marveled, and glorified God, which had given such power unto men.
Jesus didn't touch him. How was this power released? The power was released through His words. There is Life in the power of the tongue.
(I am filled with the power and the miracles and gifts of God in me. Just as Jesus did, I release the power through my words and people are liberated from bondages.
Proverbs 18:21. The power is in my tongue.

CHAPTER 4

FAVOR WITH GOD

I have two-dimensional favor. I have favor with God and I have favor with man.

Psalms 8:5 "Thou hast ... crowned him (me) with glory & honor."

John 17:22 "The glory which Thou gavest Me I have given them."
(I have the same glory Jesus has. I live expecting good things to happen to me today.)

John 12:26 "If any man serve Me ... him will My Father honor."
(I serve Jesus. My God honors and favors ME!)

Numbers 6:25 "The Lord make His face to shine upon thee, and be gracious unto thee."

(God favors me today. God honors me today. I am a success today. I have God's special favor upon me today. I am someone very special with the Lord. I have a spirit of success and achievement!)

Ephesians 3:16-20 God has granted unto me that I be strengthened with might by His Spirit in my inner man; Christ is dwelling in my heart by faith; I am rooted & grounded in love, I do comprehend and know the love of Christ, I am filled with all the fullness of God; He is able to do exceeding abundantly above all that I ask or think, according to the power that works in me. His mighty power is taking over in me.

Luke 1:37 For with God nothing shall be impossible. For with God all things are possible.

Matthew 17:20 If you have faith as a grain of mustard seed...nothing shall be impossible with you.

Zechariah 12:10 I will pour upon the house of David the spirit of grace & supplications.
(Grace is undeserved favor. God is pouring out upon me today the spirit of His favor.)

Romans 5:17 I am reigning in this life as a king through Jesus Christ. I expect something great to happen to me today.

Luke 2:40 The child grew, and waxed strong in spirit, filled with wisdom: and the grace of God was upon Him.
(I am strong in spirit, I am filled with wisdom, the favor of God is on me right now.)

Daniel 1:9 Now God had brought Daniel into favor and tender love with the prince of the eunuchs.
(Just as the Lord brought Daniel into favor & success, He is also bringing me into favor and success. I live excited! I live expecting miracles to flow. God in me makes me a success.)

Genesis 39:4-6 Joseph found favor in Potiphar's sight, and he served him. Then he made him overseer of his house, and all that he had he put under his authority.
(What God did for Joseph He will do for me. I have favor with my employer, my customers/clients, and associates and co-workers.)

Genesis 39:21 The Lord was with Joseph, and showed him mercy, and gave him favor in the sight of the keeper of the prison.

Esther 2:15 Esther obtained favor in the sight of all them that looked upon her.
(I shall have favor with people today. I will meet nice people today. I shall have good relationships with people today. I shall favor and honor others today. I rid myself of any negative spirit and attitude. A negative spirit or attitude will short circuit Gods favor to me.)

Psalms 86:15 But thou O Lord are a God full of compassion, and gracious, long suffering, and plenteous in mercy and truth.

Proverbs 23:7 As a man thinks in his heart, so is he.
(The thing that you keep thinking on and meditating on will soon be in your front yard - for good or bad, positive or negative. Keep your thoughts positive.)

CHAPTER 5

THE PRE-EXISTENCE OF JESUS CHRIST
or, THE PRE-INCARNATE CHRIST

These scriptures show that Jesus existed before he was born of Mary, who was a virgin.

John 1:1 In the beginning was the Word, and the Word was with God, and the Word was God.
John 1:2 The same was in the beginning with God.
John 1:3 All things were made by Him: and without Him was not anything made that was made.
John 1:4 In Him was LIFE; and the LIFE was the LIGHT of men.
John 1:5 And the LIGHT shineth in darkness, and the darkness comprehended it not.
John 1:14 And the Word was made flesh, and dwelt (tabernacled) among us.

1 John 1:1 He who was from the beginning, Whom we have heard, whom we have seen with our eyes, whom we have looked upon, and our hands have handled, of the Word of LIFE;
...(our hands have handled something that was from the beginning!)
1 John 1:2 For the (Word of) LIFE was manifested (made flesh), and we have seen it, and bear witness, and show (proclaim) unto you that Eternal Life, which was with the Father, and was manifested unto us.
1 Timothy 3:16 ... God was manifest in the flesh.

Hebrews 2:14 Forasmuch then as the children are partakers of flesh and blood, He also Himself likewise took part of the same (flesh and blood); so that through His death He might destroy him that had the power of death, that is, the devil...

Isaiah 7:14 Therefore the Lord Himself shall give you a sign; Behold a virgin shall conceive, and bear a son, and shall call His name Immanuel.

Matthew 1:20 " ... Joseph, thou son of David, fear not to take unto thee Mary thy wife: for that which is conceived in her is of the Holy Ghost.
Matthew 1:21 "And she shall bring forth a son, and thou shalt call His name Jesus: for He shall save His people from their sins."

Matthew 1:22 Now all this was done, that it might be fulfilled which was spoken of the Lord by the prophet, saying,
Matthew 1:23 "Behold, a virgin shall be with child, and shall bring forth a son, and they shall call His name Emmanuel," which being interpreted is, God with us.

Isaiah 9:6 For unto us a child is born, unto us a son is given: and the government shall be upon His shoulder: and His name shall be called Wonderful Counselor, the mighty God, the Everlasting Father, The Prince of Peace.

Colossians 1:17 And He is before all things, and by Him all things consist (hold together). 18 ...He is the beginning, the firstborn from the dead...

John 17:5 Jesus Himself said: "And now, O Father, glorify thou Me with thine own self with the glory which I had with thee before the world was.
John 17:24 "... for You loved Me before the foundation of the world."

Micah 5:2 ... out of thee shall He come forth unto Me that is to be ruler in Israel; whose goings forth have been of old, from everlasting.

Daniel 7:9 I beheld till the thrones were cast down, and the Ancient of Days did sit, whose garment was white as snow, and the hair of his head was like the pure wool: his throne was like the fiery flame, and his wheels as burning fire.
Revelation 1:14 His head and his hairs were white like wool, as white as snow; and his eyes were as a flame of fire.

Revelation 1:8 I am Alpha and Omega, the beginning and the ending, saith the Lord, which is, and which was, and which is to come, the Almighty.

Psalms 102:24 ...Thy years are throughout all generations.

Psalms 102:25 Of old thou hast laid the foundation of the earth, and the heavens are the work of thy hands.

Hebrews 1:2 God ... hath in these last days spoken unto us by His Son, whom He hath appointed heir of all things, by whom also He made the worlds,
Hebrews 1:3 Who being the brightness (radiance) of His glory, and the express image (exact representation) of his person (nature), and upholding all things by the word of His power, when He had by Himself purged our sins, sat down on the right hand of the majesty on high.

John 6:38 For I came down from heaven, not to do my own will, but the will of Him who sent Me.

John 16:28 I came forth from the Father, and am come into the world; again I leave the world, and go to the Father.

Philippians 2:5-11 Have this attitude in yourselves which was also in Christ Jesus,

6 Who, although He existed in the form of God, did not regard equality with God a thing to be grasped,
7 but emptied Himself (laid aside His privileges and rights), taking the form of a bond-servant, and being made in the likeness of men.
8 And being found in appearance as a man, He humbled Himself by becoming obedient to the point of death, even death on a cross.
9 Therefore also God highly exalted Him, and bestowed on Him the name which is above every name,
10 that at the name of Jesus every knee should bow, of those who are in heaven, and on earth, and under the earth,
11 And that every tongue should confess that Jesus Christ is Lord, to the glory of God the Father.

1 Peter 1:20 Who verily was foreordained before the foundation of the world, but was manifest in these last times for you.

EXODUS CHAPTER 3 – MOSES AND THE BURNING BUSH

Exodus 3:13-14 When I say to them, "The God of your fathers has sent me to you," and they shall say to me, "What is his name?", what shall I say unto them?
14 And God said unto Moses, "I AM THAT I AM": and He said, "Thus shalt thou say unto the children of Israel, I AM has sent me unto you."
John 8:56 Your father Abraham rejoiced to see my day: and he saw it, and was glad.
John 8:58 Verily I say to you, Before Abraham was, I AM.

1 Corinthians 10:4 And did all drink the same spiritual drink: for they drank of that spiritual Rock that followed them: and that Rock was Christ.
1 Corinthians 10:9 Neither let us tempt Christ, as some of them also tempted, and were destroyed of serpents.
Acts 7:38 This is he (Moses), that was in the church in the wilderness with the Angel which spoke to him in the mount Sinai, and with our fathers…

JESUS IS THE ANGEL OF THE LORD

Genesis 16:7 And the angel of the LORD found her (Hagar) by a fountain of water in the wilderness, by the fountain in the way to Shur.

Genesis 22:11 And the angel of the LORD called unto him out of heaven, and said, Abraham, Abraham: and he said, Here am I.
Genesis 22:12 And he said, Lay not thine hand upon the lad, neither do thou anything unto him: for now I know that thou fearest God, seeing thou hast not withheld thy son, thine only son from me.

EXODUS CHAPTER 3 - MOSES AND THE ANGEL OF THE LORD

Exodus 3:4 And when the LORD saw that he turned aside to see, God called unto him out of the midst of the bush, and said, Moses, Moses. And he said, Here am I.

Exodus 14:19 And the angel of God, which went before the camp of Israel, removed and went behind them; and the pillar of the cloud went from before their face, and stood behind them:

Exodus 40: 34 Then a cloud covered the tent of the congregation, and the glory of the LORD filled the tabernacle.
Exodus 40:35 And Moses was not able to enter into the tent of the congregation, because the cloud abode thereon, and the glory of the LORD filled the tabernacle.
Exodus 40:38 For the cloud of the LORD was upon the tabernacle by day, and fire was on it by night, in the sight of all the house of Israel, throughout all their journeys.

Numbers 22:22 And God's anger was kindled because he (Balaam) went: and the angel of the LORD stood in the way for an adversary against him.
Numbers 22:23 And the donkey saw the angel of the LORD standing in the way, and his sword drawn in his hand: and the donkey turned aside out of the way, and went into the field: and Balaam smote the donkey to turn her into the way.

Judges 2:1 And an angel of the LORD came up from Gilgal to Bochim, and said, I made you to go up out of Egypt, and have brought you unto the land which I sware unto your fathers; and I said, I will never break my covenant with you.
Judges 2:4 And it came to pass, when the angel of the LORD spake these words unto all the children of Israel, that the people lifted up their voice, and wept.
Judges 6:21 Then the angel of the LORD put forth the end of the staff that was in his hand, and touched the flesh and the unleavened cakes; and there rose up fire out of the rock, and consumed the flesh and the unleavened cakes. Then the angel of the LORD departed out of his sight.

Judges 13:6 Then the woman came and told her husband, saying, A man of God came unto me, and his countenance was like the countenance of an angel of God, very terrible: but I asked him not whence he was, neither told he me his name:
Judges 13:19 So Manoah took a kid with a meat offering, and offered it upon a rock unto the LORD: and the angel did wondrously; and Manoah and his wife looked on.
Judges 13:20 For it came to pass, when the flame went up toward heaven from off the altar, that the angel of the LORD ascended in the flame of the altar. And Manoah and his wife looked on it, and fell on their faces to the ground.

CHAPTER 6

SALVATION SCRIPTURES

Here are Bible verses that have been put together to show you God's free love gift for you. God is giving you a free gift called Eternal Life. Will you receive this free gift? The word "gospel" means "good news." God is giving you good news today. I pray that you have faith to believe and trust God's word written here so that you may receive God's Eternal Life.

John 3:16-21 For God so loved the world, that He gave His only begotten Son, that whosoever believeth in Him should not perish, but have everlasting life.

17 For God sent not His Son into the world to condemn the world; but that the world through Him might be saved.

18 He that believeth on Him is not condemned: but he that believeth not is condemned already, because he has not believed in the Name of the only begotten Son of God.

19 And this is the condemnation: that Light is come into the world, and men loved darkness rather than light, because their deeds were evil.

20 For every one that doeth evil hates the light, neither comes to the light, lest his deeds should be reproved.

21 But he that doeth truth comes to the light, that his deeds may be made manifest, that they are wrought in God.

John 3:36 He that believes on the Son has everlasting life: and he that believes not the son shall not see life; but the wrath of God abides on him.

John 3:3 Jesus answered and said unto him, "Unless a man be born again, he cannot see the kingdom of God."

John 3:5 Jesus answered, "Verily, verily, I say unto you, unless a man be born of water and of the Spirit, he cannot enter into the kingdom of God.

John 3:6 That which is born of the flesh is flesh; and that which is born of the Spirit is spirit."

Luke 4:18 The Spirit of the Lord is upon me, because He has anointed me to preach the gospel to the poor, He has sent me to heal the brokenhearted, to preach deliverance to the captives, and recovering of sight to the blind, to set at liberty them that are bruised,

Luke 4:19 To preach the acceptable year of the Lord.

JESUS IS GOD

Revelation 1:8 I am Alpha and Omega, the beginning and the ending, saith the Lord, which is, and which was, and which is to come, the Almighty.

JESUS IS THE CREATOR

John 1:1-5, 10-14 In the beginning was the Word, and the Word was with God, and the Word was God.

2 The same was in the beginning with God.

3 All things were made by Him: and without Him was not anything made that was made.

4 In Him was life; and the life was the light of men.

5 And the light shines in darkness; and the darkness comprehended it not.

10 He was in the world, and the world was made by Him, and the world knew Him not.

11 He came unto His own, and His own received Him not.

12 But as many as received Him, to them He gave power to become the sons of God, even to them that believe on His name:

13 Which were born, not of blood, nor of the will of the flesh, nor of the will of man, but [which were born] of God.

14 And the Word was made flesh and dwelt among us...

JESUS IS THE SON OF GOD

John 3:16 For God so loved the world that He gave His only begotten Son ...
John 6:68 Then Simon Peter answered Him, "Lord, to whom shall we go? Thou hast the words of eternal life.
John 6:69 And we believe and are sure that thou art that Christ, the Son of the living God."

JESUS IS THE LAMB OF GOD

John 1:29 The next day John seeth Jesus coming unto him, and saith, "Behold the Lamb of God, which taketh away the sin of the world."

JESUS IS THE SAVIOR

John 3:17 For God sent not His Son into the world to condemn the world; but that the world through Him might be saved.

SALVATION IS THROUGH JESUS

When a person is born, a birth certificate is written up to record their birth. When a person is BORN AGAIN, a Birth Certificate is written up to record their NEW BIRTH in the Book of Life of the Lamb (Revelation 13:8) and whosoever was not found written in the Book of Life was cast into the lake of fire. (Revelation 20:15)

Matthew 11:28-30 Come unto Me, all ye that labor and are heavy laden, and I will give you rest.
29 Take My yoke upon you, and learn of Me; for I am meek and lowly in heart: and ye shall find rest unto your souls.
30 For My yoke is easy, and My burden is light.

John 6:37-40 All that the Father giveth me shall come to me; and him that cometh to me I will in no wise cast out.
38 For I came down from heaven, not to do mine own will, but the will of Him that sent me.
39 And this is the Father's will which hath sent me: that of all which He hath given me I should lose nothing, but should raise it up again at the last day.
40 And this is the will of Him that sent me: that everyone which seeth the Son, and believeth on Him, may have everlasting life: and I will raise him up at the last day.

Matthew 5:3-6 Blessed are the poor in spirit: for theirs is the kingdom of Heaven.
4 Blessed are they that mourn: for they shall be comforted.
5 Blessed are the meek: for they shall inherit the earth.
6 Blessed are they which do hunger and thirst after righteousness: for they shall be filled.

John 14:6 I am the Way, the Truth, and the Life: no man cometh unto the Father, but by Me.

John 10:9-10 I am the door: by Me if any man enter in, he shall be saved...

10 The thief cometh not but for to steal, kill and destroy: I am come that they might have life, and have it more abundantly.

Philippians 2:9-11 Wherefore God also hath highly exalted Him, and given Him a name which is above every name:
10 That at the name of Jesus every knee should bow, of things in heaven, and things in earth, and things under the earth;
11 And that every tongue should confess that Jesus Christ is Lord, to the glory of God the Father.

Acts 4:12 Neither is there salvation in any other: for there is none other name under Heaven given among men, whereby we must be saved.

1 John 5:10-12 ...he that believeth not God hath made Him a liar; because he believeth not the record that God gave of His Son.
11 And this is the record: that God hath given to us Eternal Life, and this Life is in His Son.
12 He that hath the Son hath life; and he that hath not the Son of God hath not life.

Revelation 3:20 Behold, I stand at the door, and knock: if any man hear my voice, and open the door, I will come in to him, and will sup with him and he with Me.

JESUS OUR REDEEMER CLEANSES US FROM SIN BY HIS BLOOD

1 Peter 1:18-19 Forasmuch as you know that you were not redeemed with corruptible things, as silver and gold,...
19 But with the precious Blood of Christ, as of a Lamb without blemish and without spot.

Revelation 1:5-6 ...Unto Him that loved us, and washed us from our sins in His own Blood,
6 And has made us kings and priests unto God and His Father...

Hebrews 9:28 So Christ was once offered to bear the sins of many, and unto them that look for Him shall He appear the second time without sin unto salvation.

Hebrews 10:17 And their sins and iniquities will I remember no more.

Ephesians 1:7 In whom we have redemption through His blood, the forgiveness of sins, according to the riches of His grace.
Acts 10:43 To Him all the prophets give witness, that through His Name whosoever believes in Him shall receive remission of sins.

Isaiah 1:18 Come now, and let us reason together, saith the Lord: though your sins be as scarlet, they shall be as white as snow.

Titus 2:14 Who gave Himself for us, that He might redeem us from all iniquity, and purify unto Himself a peculiar people, zealous of good works.
Titus 3:5 Not by works of righteousness which we have done, but according to His mercy He saved us, by the washing of regeneration, and renewing of the Holy Ghost.

BENEFITS OF BEING SAVED

2 Corinthians 5:17-19, 21 Therefore if any man be in Christ, he is a new creature: old things are passed away; behold, all things are become new.

5:18 And all things are of God, who hath reconciled us to Himself by Jesus Christ, and hath given to us the ministry of reconciliation,

5:19 To wit, that God was in Christ, reconciling the world unto Himself, not imputing their trespasses unto them; and hath committed unto us the word of reconciliation.

5.21 For He hath made Him to be sin for us, who knew no sin; that we might be made the righteousness of God in Him.

Colossians 1:13-14 Who has delivered us from the power of darkness, and has translated us into the kingdom of His dear Son;

Colossians 1:14 In whom we have redemption through His Blood, even the forgiveness of sins.

Galatians 1:4 Who gave Himself for our sins, that He might deliver us from this present evil world, according to the will of God and our Father.

Ephesians 1.13 In whom ye also [trusted], after that ye heard the word of truth, the gospel of your salvation: in whom also after that ye believed, ye were sealed with that holy Spirit of promise,

Ephesians 1.14 Which is the earnest of our inheritance until the redemption of the purchased possession, unto the praise of his glory.

Ephesians 4.30 And grieve not the holy Spirit of God, whereby ye are sealed unto the day of redemption.

Hebrews 9.12 having obtained eternal redemption [for us].

Hebrews 9.15 they which are called might receive the promise of eternal inheritance.

THE SINNER

Proverbs 13:15 The way of transgressors is hard.

Romans 3:9 All are under sin...

Romans 3:10 As it is written, There is none righteous, no, not one.

Isaiah 64:6 ...all our righteousnesses are as filthy rags.

Romans 3:23 For all have sinned, and come short of the glory of God.

Romans 6:23 For the wages of sin is death; but the gift of God is Eternal Life through Jesus Christ our Lord.

Romans 5:8 But God commendeth His love toward us, in that, while we were yet sinners, Christ died for us.

THE SINNER MUST REPENT

The sinner must turn away from their old sin life, never to return to it. Never! That is true repentance.

2 Peter 3:9 The Lord is not slack concerning His promise, as some men count slackness; but is longsuffering toward us, not willing that any should perish, but that all should come to repentance.

Matthew 9:13 Jesus said, "I am … come to call … sinners to repentance."

Luke 13:3 Unless you repent, you shall all likewise perish.

Luke 15:7 I say unto you, that likewise joy shall be in heaven over one sinner that repents, more than over 99 just persons, which need no repentance.

Luke 15:10 Likewise, I say unto you, there is joy in the presence of the angels of God over one sinner that repents.

Acts 2:38 Repent, and be baptized every one of you in the name of Jesus Christ for the remission of sins, and you shall receive the gift of the Holy Ghost.

Acts 3:19 Repent ye therefore, and be converted, that your sins may be blotted out.

Acts 17:30 But God now commands all men everywhere to repent.

Acts 3:26 Unto you first God, having raised up His Son Jesus, sent Him to bless you, in turning away every one of you from his iniquities.

Luke 19:10 For Jesus is come to seek and to save that which was lost.

John 4:23 But the hour cometh, and now is, when the true worshippers shall worship the Father in spirit and in truth: for the Father seeketh such to worship Him.

IF YOU DON'T REPENT…HELL AND WRATH IS WAITING FOR YOU

John 8:24 Jesus said, "If you believe not that I am He, you shall die in your sins."

Revelation 20:15 And whosoever was not found written in the Book of Life was cast into the lake of fire.

When you meet Jesus on Judgment Day, will He be your Savior or Judge?

If you are saved, He shall say:

Matthew 25:34 "Come, ye blessed of My Father, inherit the kingdom prepared for you from the foundation of the world."

If you are lost, He shall say:

Matthew 25:41 "Depart from Me, you cursed, into everlasting fire, prepared for the devil and his angels."

RECEIVE GOD'S FREE LOVE GIFT - JESUS

John 1:12 But as many as received Him, to them He gave power to become the sons of God, even to them that believe on His Name.

Revelation 3:20 Behold, I stand at the door and knock: if any man hears my voice, and opens the door, I will come in to him, and will sup with him, and he with Me.

Ephesians 2:8 For by grace are you saved through faith; and that [faith is] not of yourselves: it is the gift of God:

Ephesians 2:9 Not of works, lest any man should boast.

Romans 10:9 That if thou shalt confess with thy mouth that Jesus is Lord, and shalt believe in thine heart that God has raised Him from the dead, thou shalt be saved.

Romans 10:10 For with the heart man believeth unto righteousness; and with the mouth confession is made unto salvation.
Romans 10:13 For whosoever shall call upon the name of the Lord shall be saved.

2 Corinthians 6:2 Behold, now is the accepted time; behold, now is the day of salvation.
John 20:31 But these are written, that you might believe that Jesus is the Christ, the Son of God; and that believing you might have life through his name.

COMFORT

Hebrews 13:5 "I will never leave you or forsake you."
Matthew 28:20 "I am with you always, even unto the end of the world."

THE FOLLOWING ARE TAKEN FROM CHICK PUBLICATIONS TRACTS:
(Visit www.chick.com)

"If I'm going to Hell, how can I miss it and go to Heaven?"
"Christ, Who created the universe (John 1:3, Hebrews 1:2), invaded our planet in the form of a man (John 1:10), by being born of a virgin. Because He loves you, He shed His Blood for you and died on the cross, to wash away your sins. Then He arose from the dead to become your Defender; but only if you accept Him as your Lord and Savior - Then you will go to Heaven."

... from "Somebody Goofed"

If you receive Christ, you have everything to gain and nothing to lose. But to reject Him - you have nothing to gain and everything to lose.

"Being perfect, He was not subject to death, the penalty for sin, but He volunteered in man's place and took man's penalty ... death and separation from God. This way He became our Savior: Through His righteousness deposited in an overdrawn account, we are restored to fellowship with God, when we accept Christ as Master of our life." 1 Peter 1:18-19

... from "Creator or Liar"

"The devil is a created being with limited power, but Jesus Christ is God Almighty with unlimited power! Jesus loves you. That's why He came to earth to die on the cross to wash away your sins with His precious blood! Jesus Christ wants to set you free by coming into your heart ... if you let Him in, then that power is yours... The Bible says "Greater is He (Jesus) that is in you, than he (satan) that is in the world." There is a way out! Turn away from your sins and ask Jesus to come into your heart. He will save you from hell and take you to Heaven!"

... from "The Contract"

"Look. Everyone said that there were plenty of ways to Heaven. Look at all the religions. There's Buddha, Confucius and Mohammed ...They're the same as Jesus."

The Angel replied, "Their bodies are still in their graves ... They were only men! Jesus tomb is empty! He arose from the dead because He is Jehovah (YAHWEH) the Creator of the Universe."

SAY THIS PRAYER SO YOU CAN GO TO HEAVEN WHEN YOU DIE

If after reading these scriptures you are not absolutely 100% sure that you have a place reserved in Heaven for you and have been born again as Jesus said, please pray this prayer now:

"Lord Jesus, I ask you to forgive me of all my sins, and come into my heart, and make me a new person. I am willing to repent and turn from my sins. I receive you Jesus, as my Savior, and I confess with my mouth that Jesus is my Lord, and Messiah, to the Glory of God the Father. Amen."

We will all die at the appointed time. Your flesh body will die, but your spirit and soul will live forever. The question is: Where will you live after you die? You have only two choices, heaven or hell. There is no such thing as purgatory. It is found nowhere in God's word. This may be your wake-up call to become a saved, born again Christian before it is too late. Make an eternal decision now to receive Jesus and ETERNAL LIFE.

THE ALIEN ENTITY and SALVATION PRAYER

One day as I was laying on my bed praying, I told the Lord that I wanted to see Him, I wanted to see what He really looked like. I immediately got a response inside of me which was, "I'm in the Book. You can see what I look like there."

So, in response to what I heard, I started looking through my Bible and I was astonished to see such descriptive language about how God looked when He appeared to people. Following are some examples.

In the book of the prophet Ezekiel, the prophet is entertaining guests in his home in Babylon, when God appears before him and transports him to Jerusalem.

In Ezekiel 8.2, Ezekiel reports: Then I beheld, and lo a likeness as the appearance of fire: from the appearance of his loins even downward, fire; and from his loins even upward, as the appearance of brightness, as the color of amber.

The color of amber is a golden yellow color, the same color as liquid, molten metal being poured from a furnace.

In chapter one of Ezekiel, he sees the throne of God coming down from Heaven, with fire enfolding the throne, with lightning and thunder, and a tornadic firenado. It was a very impressive and awesome sight! The throne was blue with a man sitting upon it. The man on the throne was the same that appeared in his home...legs of fire and a torso of amber.

Who is this entity? This is Jesus before he took on a flesh and blood body and was born of a virgin.

Moses was tending the sheep when God appeared to him as a large flame of fire in a burning bush. The bush was engulfed in flames but was not destroyed. This is also Jesus before he took on a flesh and blood body.

Later, on Mount Sinai, God came down in a flame of fire, with the mountain smoking like a furnace, with ear-piercing trumpet blasts and the booming voice of God, thunder and lightning flashes, with the mountain experiencing an earthquake. God met with Moses and the elders of Israel and they had supper with Jehovah God Almighty there on the mountaintop. Yes, this too, is a description of Jesus before he took on a flesh and blood body and was born of a virgin. Jesus is the Almighty God! Jesus is Jehovah, or Yahweh, however you want to spell it.

Later, God was manifest in the flesh and walked among mankind. It is recorded in the Bible that when Jesus went to the top of a mountain with the apostles Peter, James and John, that His Divine Nature was revealed.
Matthew 17:2 And was transfigured before them: and his face did shine as the sun, and his raiment was white as the light.
This is Jesus Christ, the same being that appeared to Ezekiel and Moses, that the prophet Daniel saw (in Daniel chapter 7), and that walked with Adam and Eve in the Garden of Eden.

Jesus was, and still is the manifestation of Love and Grace. He volunteered to come down to this place called Earth, become an offering for our sins, and take away our sin and disease. Jesus is God's free love gift to us. Believe it. FEAR NOT! Receive Him into your heart so you can be granted eternal salvation and be rescued from an eternity in hell.

Where Will You Live After You Die?

You will live forever. Did you know that?
No, not your physical body that you live in. Your body is not the real you. The real "you" is your spirit and soul, your personality, thoughts, feelings and emotions... which lives in your human body. Your human spirit and soul will live forever somewhere...but where?
So the question remains, where will you live after you die?
Some think that because their parents were a certain religion, or devoutly followed a religious tradition, or was baptized as an infant, that will guarantee them a place in Heaven. Not true.
No amount of good works or prayers to the saints or Blessed Virgin can get you into Heaven.
What makes you think that the Heavenly Father God will allow you into Heaven?

Neither will going to a church, or doing good deeds, or being good enough or buying your way in. Nope! No amount of money or being good enough can get you into Heaven. If all that were true, then Jesus Christ came down from Heaven and died on the cross in vain... all for nothing.

If you want to join a club or organization, you must sign-up, or enroll, and pay the membership fee. Only then will you be granted access. Gate crashers are not allowed in.

If you want to live in Heaven after you die, you must enroll first, and the membership fee must be paid. The membership fee is extremely expensive. That fee to get in is the blood of God's son, Jesus Christ. By his shed blood He provided a bundle of benefits. Jesus offered Himself on the cross as a living sacrifice to pay for your salvation, your healing, and your righteousness with God.

Your name must be written in Heaven <u>before</u> you die. But the catch is that your membership fee has already been paid on your behalf as a free love gift to you. What you need to do is believe it and receive it. If you <u>do not believe</u> and receive it, you are <u>rejecting</u> God's Son. If you reject God's Son, you are rejecting God! The only place for those folks is to live in hell with the devil and his evil demons. That is NOT God's plan for you.
John 3:18 Jesus said: He that believeth on him is not condemned: but he that believeth not is <u>condemned already</u>, because he hath not believed in the name of the only begotten Son of God.
John 3:19 And this is the condemnation, that light is come into the world, and men loved
    darkness rather than light, because their deeds were evil.

Do You Want to Live Forever with God?

Jesus has made a way for you to be set free from the devil. Jesus said the devil is a liar, a deceiver, and a murderer.
If you are not sure whether you have a place reserved in heaven, you should make your reservation now.
If you receive Jesus, you have everything to gain and nothing to lose. But if you reject Him, you have *nothing* to gain and *everything* to lose.
My friend, Jesus loves you and cares for you. Had it not been for the grace of God, the devil would have killed you long ago. God is giving you a chance to get saved. Jesus loves you. That's why He came to earth and died on the cross to wash away your sins with His precious Blood! Jesus Christ the Messiah wants to set you free by coming into your heart.
If you pray this prayer with an honest, sincere heart, Jesus will hear you and will definitely save you from Hell and make you a child of God and take you to heaven when you die.

Pray This Prayer to Go to Heaven

"Lord Jesus, I ask you to forgive me of all my sins, and come into my heart, and make me a new person. I do repent right now and turn away from my sins. I receive you Jesus, as my Savior, and I confess with my mouth that Jesus is my Lord, and Messiah, to the Glory of God the Father. Amen."
If you have prayed this prayer and sincerely mean it, then the angels are rejoicing!

Your Assurance of Salvation

John 3:3 Jesus answered and said unto him, Verily, verily I say unto thee, Except a man be born again, he cannot see the kingdom of God.

John 3:4 Nicodemus saith unto him. How can a man be born when he is old? Can he enter the second time into his mother's womb, and be born?

John 3:5 Jesus answered, Verily, verily, I say unto thee, Except a man be born of water and of the spirit, he cannot enter into the kingdom of God.

John 3:6 That which is born of the flesh is flesh; and that which is born of the Spirit is spirit.

John 3:7 Marvel not that I said unto thee, Ye must be born again.

John 3:16 For God so loved the world that he gave his only begotten Son, that whosoever believeth in him should not perish, but have everlasting life.

John 3:17 For God sent not his Son into the world to condemn the world: but that the world through him might be saved.

John 3:18 He that believeth on him is not condemned: but he that believeth not is condemned already, because he hath not believed in the name of the only begotten Son of God.

John 3:19 And this is the condemnation, that light is come into the world, and men loved darkness rather than light, because their deeds were evil.

John 3:20 For every one that doeth evil hateth the light, neither cometh to the light, lest his deeds should be reproved.

John 3:21 But he that doeth truth cometh to the light, that his deeds may be manifest, that they are wrought in God.

John 1:10 He (Jesus) was in the world, and the world was made by him, and the world knew him not.

John 1:11 He came unto his own, and his own received him not.

John 1:12 But as many as received him, to them gave he power to become the sons of God, even to them that believe on his name.

Colossians 1:12-14 Giving thanks unto the Father, which hath made us able to be partakers of the inheritance of the saints in light:

1:13 Who hath delivered us from the power of darkness, and hath translated us into the kingdom of his dear Son:

1:14 In whom we have redemption through his blood, even the forgiveness of sins.

Luke 13:3 I tell you, Nay: But, except ye repent, ye shall all likewise perish.

John 8:24 I said therefore unto you, that ye shall die in your sins: for if you believe not that I am He, ye shall die in your sins.

Ephesians 2:8-9 For by grace are ye saved through faith: and that not of yourselves: it is the gift of God.

2:9 Not of works, lest any man should boast.

Romans 10: 9 That if thou shalt confess with thy mouth the Lord Jesus, and shalt believe in thine heart that God hath raised him from the dead, thou shall be saved.

Romans 10:10 For with the heart man believeth unto righteousness; and with the mouth confession is made unto salvation.
Romans 10:13 For whosoever shall call upon the name of the Lord shall be saved.

John 14:6 Jesus saith unto him, I am the way, the truth, and the life: no man cometh unto the Father, but by me.

Philippians 2:9-11 Wherefore God also hath highly exalted him, and given him a name which is above every name:
2:10 That at the name of Jesus every knee should bow, of things in heaven, and things in earth, and things under the earth;
2:11 And that every tongue should confess that Jesus Christ is Lord, to the glory of God the Father.

Acts 4:12 Neither is there salvation in any other: for there is none other name under heaven given among men, whereby we must be saved.

NOT The End,
BUT the beginning of a new life in Jesus Christ!

CHAPTER 7

WATER BAPTISM IS A "MUST"!

There are many modern-day Christian churches who do not emphasize the necessity of water baptism, even though Jesus and the apostles said it is a MUST, as we will see in the scriptures listed below.

Acts 2:37 Now when they heard this, they were pricked in their heart, and said unto Peter and to the rest of the apostles, Men and brethren, <u>what shall we do</u>?
Acts 2:38 Then Peter said unto them, <u>Repent, and be baptized</u> every one of you in the name of Jesus Christ for the <u>remission of sins</u>, and ye shall receive the gift of the Holy Ghost.

Without water baptism, Romans chapter six makes no sense and the believer will fall ever more into the deeds of the "old man." See Romans 6:4: Therefore we are buried with him by <u>baptism</u> into death: that like as Christ was raised up from the dead by the glory of the Father, even so we also should walk in newness of life.

Matthew 28:19 Jesus commanded: Go ye therefore, and teach all nations, <u>baptizing</u> them in the name of the Father, and of the Son, and of the Holy Ghost:

In the Old Testament, or Old Covenant, (Old Contract), the sign or mark of being in covenant with God was circumcision. In the New Testament, or New Covenant, (New Contract), the sign or mark of being in covenant with God is the water baptism of repentance. To repent means to make a firm decision to NEVER, EVER turn back to any of your sins. It means turn your back on your old sin life and NEVER go back to your sins. Not just for a day, or week or a month, but forever.

A supernatural "circumcision made without hands" occurs under the waters of baptism. It marks our hearts for God and the pull of sin decreases, though it is there from time to time seeking to tempt and destroy us. But do not allow your defeated enemy to control you. Jesus destroyed sin and satan. Get water baptized and receive the baptism in the Holy Spirit with the evidence of speaking in tongues. Speaking in tongues is a heavenly prayer language where the Holy Spirit in you is speaking directly to your heavenly Father God, praying and interceding for you. See Romans 8:26-28.

Also, before you get water baptized, expect a miracle or supernatural event or manifestation to happen during or soon after. Pray for your spiritual eyes to be opened. Expect miracles!

It happened at the baptism of Jesus and also the Ethiopian eunuch in Acts 8:36-38.

Colossians 2:9-15 For in him dwelleth all the fulness of the Godhead bodily.
2:10 And ye are complete in him, which is the head of all principality and power:
2:11 In whom also ye are circumcised with the circumcision made without hands, in putting off the body of the sins of the flesh by the circumcision of Christ:
2:12 Buried with him in baptism, wherein also ye are risen with him through the faith of the operation of God, who hath raised him from the dead.
2:13 And you, being dead in your sins and the uncircumcision of your flesh, hath he quickened together with him, having forgiven you all trespasses;
2:14 Blotting out the handwriting of ordinances that was against us, which was contrary to us, and took it out of the way, nailing it to his cross;
2:15 And having spoiled principalities and powers, he made a shew of them openly, triumphing over them in it.

BAPTISM

Mark 1:4 John did baptize in the wilderness, and preach the baptism of repentance for the remission of sins.
Luke 3:3 And he came into all the country about Jordan, preaching the baptism of repentance for the remission of sins;
Luke 7:29 And all the people that heard him, and the publicans, justified God, being baptized with the baptism of John.
Luke 12:50 But I have a baptism to be baptized with; and how am I straitened till it be accomplished!
Luke 20:4 The baptism of John, was it from heaven, or of men?
Acts 10:37 That word, I say, ye know, which was published throughout all Judaea, and began from Galilee, after the baptism which John preached;
Acts 13:24 When John had first preached before his coming the baptism of repentance to all the people of Israel.
Acts 18:25 This man was instructed in the way of the Lord; and being fervent in the spirit, he spake and taught diligently the things of the Lord, knowing only the baptism of John.
Acts 19:3 And he said unto them, Unto what then were ye baptized? And they said, Unto John's baptism.

Acts 19:4 Then said Paul, John verily baptized with the baptism of repentance, saying unto the people, that they should believe on him which should come after him, that is, on Christ Jesus.

Romans 6:4 Therefore we are buried with him by baptism into death: that like as Christ was raised up from the dead by the glory of the Father, even so we also should walk in newness of life.

Ephesians 4:5 One Lord, one faith, one baptism,

Colossians 2:12 Buried with him in baptism, wherein also ye are risen with him through the faith of the operation of God, who hath raised him from the dead.

1 Peter 3:21 The like figure whereunto even baptism doth also now save us (not the putting away of the filth of the flesh, but the answer of a good conscience toward God,) by the resurrection of Jesus Christ:

BAPTIZE

Matthew 3:11 I indeed baptize you with water unto repentance: but he that cometh after me is mightier than I, whose shoes I am not worthy to bear: he shall baptize you with the Holy Ghost, and with fire:

Mark 1:4 John did baptize in the wilderness, and preach the baptism of repentance for the remission of sins.

BAPTIZED

Matthew 3:6 And were baptized of him in Jordan, confessing their sins.

Mark 1:5 And there went out unto him all the land of Judaea, and they of Jerusalem, and were all baptized of him in the river of Jordan, confessing their sins.

Mark 16:16 Jesus said: He that believeth and is baptized shall be saved; but he that believeth not shall be damned.

Acts 1:5 Jesus said:For John truly baptized with water; but ye shall be baptized with the Holy Ghost not many days hence.

Acts 2:38 Then Peter said unto them, Repent, and be baptized every one of you in the name of Jesus Christ for the remission of sins, and ye shall receive the gift of the Holy Ghost.

Acts 2:41 Then they that gladly received his word were baptized: and the same day there were added unto them about three thousand souls.

Acts 8:12 But when they believed Philip preaching the things concerning the kingdom of God, and the name of Jesus Christ, they were baptized, both men and women.

Acts 8:13 Then Simon himself believed also: and when he was baptized, he continued with Philip, and wondered, beholding the miracles and signs which were done.

Acts 8:16 (For as yet he was fallen upon none of them: only they were baptized in the name of the Lord Jesus.)

Acts 8:36 And as they went on their way, they came unto a certain water: and the eunuch said, See, here is water; what doth hinder me to be baptized?

Acts 8:38 And he commanded the chariot to stand still: and they went down both into the water, both Philip and the eunuch; and he baptized him.

Acts 9:18 And immediately there fell from his (Saul of Tarsus) eyes as it had been scales: and he received sight forthwith, and arose, and was baptized.

Acts 10:47 Can any man forbid water, that these should not be <u>baptized</u>, which have received the Holy Ghost as well as we?

Acts 10:48 And he commanded them to be <u>baptized</u> in the name of the Lord. Then prayed they him to tarry certain days.

Acts 11:16 Then remembered I the word of the Lord, how that he said, John indeed <u>baptized</u> with water; but ye shall be baptized with the Holy Ghost.

Acts 16:15 And when she was <u>baptized</u>, and her household, she besought us, saying, If ye have judged me to be faithful to the Lord, come into my house, and abide there. And she constrained us.

Acts 16:33 And he took them the same hour of the night, and washed their stripes; and was <u>baptized</u>, he and all his, straightway.

Acts 18:8 And Crispus, the chief ruler of the synagogue, believed on the Lord with all his house; and many of the Corinthians hearing believed, and were <u>baptized</u>.

Acts 19:3 And he said unto them, Unto what then were ye <u>baptized</u>? And they said, Unto John's <u>baptism</u>.

Acts 19:4 Then said Paul, John verily <u>baptized</u> with the <u>baptism of repentance</u>, saying unto the people, that they should believe on him which should come after him, that is, on Christ Jesus.

Acts 19:5 When they heard this, they were <u>baptized</u> in the name of the Lord Jesus.

Acts 22:16 And now why tarriest thou? arise, and be <u>baptized</u>, and <u>wash away thy sins,</u> calling on the name of the Lord.

Romans 6:3 Know ye not, that so many of us as were <u>baptized</u> into Jesus Christ were <u>baptized</u> into his death?

Galatians 3:27 For as many of you as have been <u>baptized</u> into Christ have put on Christ.

CHAPTER 8

ALL THE SCRIPTURES YOU NEED TO KNOW ABOUT THE BAPTISM IN THE HOLY SPIRIT AND PRAYING IN OTHER TONGUES – A STUDY GUIDE –

Don't let anyone tell you that the Holy Spirit, speaking in tongues, healings and miracles and other manifestations of God are not for today, or not from God, or any other nonsense. The devil is speaking through them. Would the devil lie to you? He was a liar from the beginning.

Speaking in tongues is your private prayer language straight to God. You do not understand the words you are saying. This prayer language is coming straight from your "spirit man", so to speak.

You are made of three parts: spirit, soul and body. Your spirit is what gets "born again" when you receive Jesus and His free love gift to you, His works of redemption on the cross.

Your soul is your mind, will and emotions, located in your head, your brain.

Your body is the fleshly home that keeps spirit and soul together, it is where you live. Your body is not you. Your spirit and soul which make up your entire personality, that is YOU.

This is a study guide. Study it along with your Bible near you. Look up the Bible passages for yourself.

I have been a saved, born again Christian since July 30, 1972. I received the Holy Spirit later that year in December of 1972. I have prayed in tongues every day since. It is what has helped me survive through many difficult trials, traumas and tribulations.

THIS IS WHAT JESUS SAYS ABOUT PRAYING FOR THE HOLY SPIRIT

Luke 11:11 If a son shall ask bread of any of you that is a father, will he give him a stone? or if he ask a fish, will he for a fish give him a serpent?
Luke 11:12 Or if he shall ask an egg, will he offer him a scorpion?
Luke 11:13 If ye then, being evil, know how to give good gifts unto your children: how much more shall your heavenly Father give the Holy Spirit to them that ask him?

Please pray and ask God for the baptism of the Holy Spirit with the evidence of speaking in tongues. Get in a quiet place, preferably where you have peace and quiet, and get alone with God. Think of what He has done for you, He has saved you from a life of sin and eternity in hell. Praise and worship Him with all your heart, sing love songs to Him, and then pray this:

"Heavenly Father, I'm asking You to save me right now and fill me with your Holy Spirit. I receive Jesus as my Savior and Lord. I receive the free love gift that You have given me through Jesus which is my redemption from sin and hellfire. Jesus' precious blood has redeemed me and washed me clean from my sins. Because of this I am asking for the infilling of your Holy Spirit with the evidence of praying in tongues, my heavenly prayer language."

Now, act on your faith and say whatever syllables come up from your heart. That's what I did. James 2:20 and 2:26 says "faith without works is dead." It may sound foolish, that's okay. Say the words you get and press through any barriers through faith and believing His Word is true and keep on till the dam breaks and you have a free-flowing prayer language.

Some people get their prayer language immediately. It took me about four months, only because the enemy, knowing I was a "baby Christian," wanted to derail and destroy me before I even got started. I got side-tracked into the occult and was tempted to pursue psychic powers for two months. But when I learned this was evil, I repented, and continued seeking the Lord and His Holy Spirit Baptism. Thankfully I pressed in until I got it. May God bless you.

Luke 24:49 And, behold, I send the promise of my Father upon you: but tarry ye in the city of Jerusalem, until ye be endued with power from on high.

THE SPIRIT PROMISED OF THE FATHER

Isaiah 32:15 [There shall be desolation] Until the Spirit be poured upon us from on high, and the wilderness be a fruitful field, and the fruitful field be counted for a forest.

Isaiah 44:2-4 Thus saith the Lord that made thee, and formed thee from the womb, which will help thee; Fear not...
3 For I will pour water upon him that is thirsty, and floods upon the dry ground: I will pour My Spirit upon thy seed, and my blessing upon thine offspring:
4 And they shall spring up as among the grass, as willows by the water courses.

Isaiah 59:21 As for Me, this is my covenant with them, saith the Lord: My Spirit that is upon thee, and My words that I have put in thy mouth, shall not depart out of thy mouth, nor out of the mouth of thy seed, nor out of the mouth of thy seed's seed, saith the Lord, from henceforth and forever.

Ezekiel 36:27 And I will put My Spirit within you, and cause you to walk in my statutes, and you shall keep my judgments, and do them.

Acts 2:16-21 But this is that which was spoken by the prophet Joel: [taken from Joel 2:28-32]
17 And it shall come to pass in the last days, saith God, I will pour out My Spirit upon all flesh: and your sons and your daughters shall prophesy, and your young men shall see visions, and your old men shall dream dreams:
18 And on my servants and on my handmaids I will pour out in those days of my Spirit, and they shall prophesy:
19 And I will show wonders in heaven above, and signs in the earth beneath; blood, and fire and vapor of smoke:
20 The sun shall be turned into darkness, and the moon into blood, before that great and terrible day of the Lord come:
21 And it shall come to pass, that whosoever shall call on the name of the Lord shall be saved.

SCRIPTURE BASIS TO RECEIVE THE HOLY SPIRIT

Luke 24:49 And, behold, I send the promise of my Father upon you: but tarry ye in the city of Jerusalem, until you be endued with power from on high.

Acts 1:4-5 And being assembled together with them, Jesus commanded them that they should not depart from Jerusalem, but "wait for the promise of the Father, which," saith He, "you have heard of Me."
5 For John truly baptized with water: but you shall be baptized with the Holy Ghost not many days hence.

Matthew 3:11 I indeed baptize you with water unto repentance: but He that cometh after me is mightier than I, whose shoes I am not worthy to bear: He shall baptize you with the Holy Ghost, and with fire.

Acts 1:8 But you shall receive Power, after that the Holy Ghost is come upon you: and you shall be witnesses unto Me both in Jerusalem, and in all Judaea, and in Samaria, and unto the uttermost part of the earth.

Acts 2:1-4 And when the day of Pentecost was fully come, they were all with one accord in one place.
2 And suddenly there came a sound from heaven as of a rushing mighty wind, and it filled all the house where they were sitting.
3 And there appeared unto them cloven tongues like as of fire, and it sat upon each of them.
4 And they were all filled with the Holy Ghost, and began to speak with other tongues, as the Spirit gave them utterance.

Mark 16:17 And these signs shall follow them that believe: In My name shall they...speak with new tongues.

Acts 2:38-39 ...you shall receive the gift of the Holy Ghost.
39 For the promise is unto you, and to your children, and to all that are afar off, even as many as the Lord our God shall call.

Acts 10:44-46 While Peter yet spoke these words, the Holy Ghost fell on all them which heard the word.
45 ...on the Gentiles also was poured out the gift of the Holy Ghost.
46 For they heard them speak with tongues, and magnify God.

Acts 19:6 And when Paul had laid his hands upon them, the Holy Ghost came on them; and they spoke with tongues, and prophesied.

Luke 11:13 If you then, being evil, know how to give good gifts unto your children: how much more shall your heavenly Father give the Holy Spirit to them that ask Him?

WHY SPEAK IN TONGUES?

1 Corinthians 14:2 For he that speaks in an unknown tongue speaks not unto men, but unto God: for no man understands him; howbeit in the Spirit he speaks mysteries.
1 Corinthians 14:4 He that speaks in an unknown tongue edifies himself,...
1 Corinthians 14:5 I wish that you all spoke with tongues.
1 Corinthians 14:14 For if I pray in an unknown tongue, my spirit prays, but my understanding is unfruitful.
1 Corinthians 14:17 For you truly give thanks well, but the other is not edified.
1 Corinthians 14:18 I thank my God, I speak with tongues more than you all.
1 Corinthians 14:22 Wherefore tongues are for a sign,...to them that believe not: prophesying serves for them which believe.

1 Corinthians 14:39 ...forbid not to speak with tongues.

Isaiah 28:11-12 For with stammering lips and another tongue will he speak to this people.
12 To whom he said, "This is the rest wherewith you may cause the weary to rest; and this is the refreshing:" yet they would not hear.

Acts 2:11 "...we do hear them speak in our tongues the wonderful works of God."

WHAT HAPPENS WHEN YOU PRAY IN TONGUES?

John 7:37-39 Jesus said, "If any man thirst, let him come unto Me, and drink.
38 He that believes on Me, as the scripture has said, out of his belly shall flow rivers of Living Water."
39 (But this spoke He of the Spirit, which they that believe on Him should receive: for the Holy Ghost was not yet given, because that Jesus was not yet glorified).

Romans 8:26 Likewise the Spirit also helps our infirmities: for we know not what we should pray for as we ought: but the Spirit Himself makes intercession for us with groanings which cannot be uttered.
Romans 8:27 And He that searches the hearts knows what is the mind of the Spirit, because He makes intercession for the saints according to the will of God.

Jude 20-21 But you, beloved, building up yourselves on your most holy faith, praying in the Holy Ghost,
21 Keep yourselves in the love of God.

James 5:16 The effectual fervent prayer of a righteous man avails much.

THINGS THE HOLY SPIRIT WILL DO FOR YOU

The Holy Spirit is the Power of God, and that Power is living in me!

1 Corinthians 12 The Gifts of the Holy Spirit will operate in me.

Galatians 5:22 The fruit of the Holy Spirit will be manifested in me. The Gifts are for power, the fruits are for character.

John 14:16 And I will pray the Father, and He shall give you another Comforter (Helper), that He may abide with you for ever.

John 14:18 I will not leave you comfortless: I will come to you. (Jesus will come to me through the Holy Spirit.)

John 14:26 But the Comforter, which is the Holy Ghost, whom the Father will send in My name, he shall teach you all things, and bring all things to your remembrance, whatsoever I have said unto you. (The Holy Ghost comes to us in the name of Jesus, so that we may go to others in Jesus name.)

John 15:26-27 But when the Comforter is come, whom I will send unto you from the Father, even the Spirit of Truth, which proceeds from the Father, He shall testify of Me:
27 And you also shall bear witness (testify)...

John 16:12-15 I have yet many things to say unto you, but you cannot bear them now.
13 Howbeit when He, the Spirit of Truth is come, He will guide you into all truth: for He shall not speak of Himself; but whatsoever He shall hear, that shall He speak: and He will show you things to come.
14 He shall glorify Me: for He shall receive of Mine, and shall show it unto you.
15 All things that the Father has are mine: therefore I said, that He shall take of Mine, and shall show it unto you.
John 16:25 I (Holy Spirit) shall show you plainly of the Father.

John 14:20 At that day you shall know that I am in my Father, and you in Me, and I in you. (The Holy Spirit shall reveal to us that Jesus is in His Father, we are in Jesus, and Jesus is in us.)

1 John 4:4 Greater is the Holy Spirit in me than the devil in the world.

Romans 8:11 He that raised up Christ Jesus from the dead shall also enliven my mortal body by His Spirit that dwells in me.

1 Corinthians 2:12 ... we have received the Spirit of God that we might know the things that are freely given to us of God.
1 Corinthians 2:9-10 God has revealed "the things which God Has prepared for them that love Him" ... unto us by His Spirit.

Ephesians 3:3-5 Revelations and mysteries are now revealed unto His holy apostles and prophets by the Spirit. **(By speaking in tongues and interpreting we know the revealed wisdom of God.)**

1 Corinthians 2:7 We speak (in tongues) the wisdom of God in a mystery (1 Corinthians 14:2), even the hidden wisdom (Proverbs 2:7)
1 Corinthians 2:13 Which things we speak ... in the words ... which the Holy Ghost teaches...

James 3 The Holy Spirit tames our tongue.

Ephesians 6:18 The Holy Spirit enables us to do spiritual warfare and intercession.

CHAPTER 9

TITLES AND NAMES OF JESUS CHRIST

Advocate 1 John 2:1 My little children, these things write I unto you, that ye sin not. And if any man sin, we have an advocate with the Father, Jesus Christ the righteous:

Almighty Revelation 1:8 I am Alpha and Omega, the beginning and the ending, saith the Lord, which is, and which was, and which is to come, the Almighty.

Alpha and Omega Revelation 1:8 I am Alpha and Omega, the beginning and the ending, saith the Lord, which is, and which was, and which is to come, the Almighty.

Amen Revelation 3:14 And unto the angel of the church of the Laodiceans write; These things saith the Amen, the faithful and true witness, the beginning of the creation of God;

Angel Genesis 48:16 The Angel which redeemed me from all evil, bless the lads;

Exodus 23:20-21 Behold, I send an Angel before thee, to keep thee in the way, and to bring thee into the place which I have prepared. Beware of him, and obey his voice, provoke him not; for he will not pardon your transgressions: for my name [is] in him.

Angel of the Lord Exodus 3:2 And the angel of the LORD appeared unto Moses in a flame of fire out of the midst of a bush: and he looked, and, behold, the bush burned with fire, and the bush [was] not consumed.

Judges 13:15 the angel ascended in the flame on the altar before Manoah

Angel of God's presence Isaiah 63:9 he saved them, redeemed them, carried them

Apostle Hebrews 3:1 Wherefore, holy brethren, partakers of the heavenly calling, consider the Apostle and High Priest of our profession, Christ Jesus;

Arm of the Lord Isaiah 51:9 Awake, awake, put on strength, O arm of the LORD; awake, as in the ancient days, in the generations of old. [Art] thou not it that hath cut Rahab, [and] wounded the dragon?

Isaiah 53:1 Who hath believed our report? and to whom is the arm of the LORD revealed?

Author and Finisher of our faith Hebrews 12:2 Looking unto Jesus the author and finisher of [our] faith; who for the joy that was set before him endured the cross, despising the shame, and is set down at the right hand of the throne of God.

Blessed and only Potentate 1 Timothy 6:15 Which in his times he shall shew, [who is] the blessed and only Potentate, the King of kings, and Lord of lords;

Beginning of the creation of God Revelation 3:14 And unto the angel of the church of the Laodiceans write; These things saith the Amen, the faithful and true witness, the beginning of the creation of God;

A Righteous Branch Jeremiah 23:5 Behold, the days come, saith the LORD, that I will raise unto David a righteous Branch, and a King shall reign and prosper, and shall execute judgment and justice in the earth.

Zechariah 3:8 I will bring forth my servant the BRANCH.

Zechariah 6:12 Behold the man whose name [is] The BRANCH; and he shall grow up out of his place, and he shall build the temple of the LORD:

Bread of Life John 6:35, 48 I am the bread of life: he that cometh to me shall never hunger; and he that believeth on me shall never thirst.

John 6:47-48 He that believeth on me hath everlasting life….I am that bread of life.

Captain of the Lord's Hosts Joshua 5:14-15 And he said, Nay; but [as] captain of the host of the LORD am I now come. And Joshua fell on his face to the earth, and did worship, and said unto him, What saith my lord unto his servant? And the captain of the LORD'S host said unto Joshua, Loose thy shoe from off thy foot; for the place whereon thou standest [is] holy. And Joshua did so.

Captain of Salvation Hebrews 2:10 For it became him, for whom [are] all things, and by whom [are] all things, in bringing many sons unto glory, to make the captain of their salvation perfect through sufferings.

Chief Shepherd 1 Peter 5:4 And when the chief Shepherd shall appear, ye shall receive a crown of glory that fadeth not away.

Christ of God Luke 9:20 He said unto them, But whom say ye that I am? Peter answering said, The Christ of God.

Consolation of Israel Luke 2:25 And, behold, there was a man in Jerusalem, whose name [was] Simeon; and the same man [was] just and devout, waiting for the consolation of Israel: and the Holy Ghost was upon him.

Chief Cornerstone Ephesians 2:20 And are built upon the foundation of the apostles and prophets, Jesus Christ himself being the chief corner [stone];

1 Peter 2:6 Wherefore also it is contained in the scripture, Behold, I lay in Sion a chief corner stone, elect, precious: and he that believeth on him shall not be confounded.

Commander Isaiah 55:4 Behold, I have given him [for] a witness to the people, a leader and commander to the people.

Counsellor Isaiah 9:6 For unto us a child is born, unto us a son is given: and the government shall be upon his shoulder: and his name shall be called Wonderful, Counsellor, The mighty God, The everlasting Father, The Prince of Peace.

David Jeremiah 30:9 But they shall serve the LORD their God, and David their king, whom I will raise up unto them.

Dayspring Luke 1:78 Through the tender mercy of our God; whereby the dayspring from on high hath visited us,

Deliverer Romans 11:26 And so all Israel shall be saved: as it is written, There shall come out of Sion the Deliverer, and shall turn away ungodliness from Jacob:

Desire of all nations Haggai 2:7 And I will shake all nations, and the desire of all nations shall come: and I will fill this house with glory, saith the LORD of hosts.

Door John 10:7 Then said Jesus unto them again, Verily, verily, I say unto you, I am the door of the sheep.

Elect of God Isaiah 42:1 Behold my servant, whom I uphold; mine elect, [in whom] my soul delighteth; I have put my spirit upon him: he shall bring forth judgment to the Gentiles.

Emmanuel Isaiah 7:14 with Matthew 1:23 Therefore the Lord himself shall give you a sign; Behold, a virgin shall conceive, and bear a son, and shall call his name Immanuel.

Matthew 1:23 Behold, a virgin shall be with child, and shall bring forth a son, and they shall call his name Emmanuel, which being interpreted is, God with us.

Eternal Life 1 John 1:2 (For the life was manifested, and we have seen [it], and bear witness, and shew unto you that eternal life, which was with the Father, and was manifested unto us;)

1 John 5:20 And we know that the Son of God is come, and hath given us an understanding, that we may know him that is true, and we are in him that is true, [even] in his Son Jesus Christ. This is the true God, and eternal life.

Everlasting Father Isaiah 9:6 For unto us a child is born, unto us a son is given: and the government shall be upon his shoulder: and his name shall be called Wonderful, Counsellor, The mighty God, The everlasting Father, The Prince of Peace.

Faithful Witness Revelation 1:5 And from Jesus Christ, [who is] the faithful witness, [and] the first begotten of the dead, and the prince of the kings of the earth. Unto him that loved us, and washed us from our sins in his own blood,

Revelation 3:14 And unto the angel of the church of the Laodiceans write; These things saith the Amen, the faithful and true witness, the beginning of the creation of God;

First and Last Revelation 1:11 Saying, I am Alpha and Omega, the first and the last:

Revelation 2:8 And unto the angel of the church in Smyrna write; These things saith the first and the last, which was dead, and is alive;

First begotten of the dead Revelation 1:5 And from Jesus Christ, [who is] the faithful witness, [and] the first begotten of the dead, and the prince of the kings of the earth. Unto him that loved us, and washed us from our sins in his own blood,

First born of every creature Colossians 1:15 Who is the image of the invisible God, the firstborn of every creature:

Forerunner Hebrews 6:20 Whither the forerunner is for us entered, [even] Jesus, made an high priest for ever after the order of Melchisedec.

God Isaiah 40:9 O Zion, that bringest good tidings, get thee up into the high mountain; O Jerusalem, that bringest good tidings, lift up thy voice with strength; lift [it] up, be not afraid; say unto the cities of Judah, Behold your God!

John 20:28 And Thomas answered and said unto him, My Lord and my God.

God blessed for ever Romans 9:5 Whose [are] the fathers, and of whom as concerning the flesh Christ [came], who is over all, God blessed for ever. Amen.

God's fellow Zechariah 13:7 Awake, O sword, against my shepherd, and against the man [that is] my fellow, saith the LORD of hosts: smite the shepherd, and the sheep shall be scattered: and I will turn mine hand upon the little ones.

Glory of the Lord Isaiah 40:5 And the glory of the LORD shall be revealed, and all flesh shall see [it] together: for the mouth of the LORD hath spoken [it].

Good Shepherd John 10:14 I am the good shepherd, and know my [sheep], and am known of mine.

Great High Priest Hebrews 4:14 Seeing then that we have a great high priest, that is passed into the heavens, Jesus the Son of God, let us hold fast [our] profession.

Governor Matthew 2:6 And thou Bethlehem, [in] the land of Juda, art not the least among the princes of Juda: for out of thee shall come a Governor, that shall rule my people Israel.

Head of the Church Ephesians 5:23 For the husband is the head of the wife, even as Christ is the head of the church: and he is the saviour of the body.

Colossians 1:18 And he is the head of the body, the church: who is the beginning, the firstborn from the dead; that in all [things] he might have the preeminence.

Heir of all things Hebrews 1:2 Hath in these last days spoken unto us by [his] Son, whom he hath appointed heir of all things, by whom also he made the worlds;

Holy One Psalms 16:10 with Acts 2:27,31 For thou wilt not leave my soul in hell; neither wilt thou suffer thine Holy One to see corruption.

Acts 2:27 Because thou wilt not leave my soul in hell, neither wilt thou suffer thine Holy One to see corruption. Vs 31: He seeing this before spake of the resurrection of Christ, that his soul was not left in hell, neither his flesh did see corruption.

Holy One of God Mark 1:24 Saying, Let [us] alone; what have we to do with thee, thou Jesus of Nazareth? art thou come to destroy us? I know thee who thou art, the Holy One of God.

Holy One of Israel Isaiah 41:14 Fear not, thou worm Jacob, [and] ye men of Israel; I will help thee, saith the LORD, and thy redeemer, the Holy One of Israel.

Horn of salvation Luke 1:69 And hath raised up an horn of salvation for us in the house of his servant David;

I Am Exodus 3:14 with John 8:58 And God said unto Moses, I AM THAT I AM: and he said, Thus shalt thou say unto the children of Israel, I AM hath sent me unto you.

John 8:58 Jesus said unto them, Verily, verily, I say unto you, Before Abraham was, I am.

Jehovah Isaiah 26:4 Trust ye in the LORD for ever: for in the LORD JEHOVAH [is] everlasting strength:

Jesus Matthew 1:21; And she shall bring forth a son, and thou shalt call his name JESUS: for he shall save his people from their sins.

1 Thessalonians 1:10 And to wait for his Son from heaven, whom he raised from the dead, [even] Jesus, which delivered us from the wrath to come.

Judge of Israel Micah 5:1 Now gather thyself in troops, O daughter of troops: he hath laid siege against us: they shall smite the judge of Israel with a rod upon the cheek.

Just One Acts 7:52 Which of the prophets have not your fathers persecuted? and they have slain them which shewed before of the coming of the Just One; of whom ye have been now the betrayers and murderers:

King Zechariah 9:9 Rejoice greatly, O daughter of Zion; shout, O daughter of Jerusalem: behold, thy King cometh unto thee: he [is] just, and having salvation; lowly, and riding upon an ass, and upon a colt the foal of an ass.

Matthew 21:5 Tell ye the daughter of Sion, Behold, thy King cometh unto thee, meek, and sitting upon an ass, and a colt the foal of an ass.

King of Israel John 1:49 Nathanael answered and saith unto him, Rabbi, thou art the Son of God; thou art the King of Israel.

King of the Jews Matthew 2:2 Saying, Where is he that is born King of the Jews? for we have seen his star in the east, and are come to worship him.

King of Saints Revelation 15:3 And they sing the song of Moses the servant of God, and the song of the Lamb, saying, Great and marvelous [are] thy works, Lord God Almighty; just and true [are] thy ways, thou King of saints.

King of Kings 1 Timothy 6:15 Which in his times he shall shew, [who is] the blessed and only Potentate, the King of kings, and Lord of lords;

Revelation 17:14 These shall make war with the Lamb, and the Lamb shall overcome them: for he is Lord of lords, and King of kings: and they that are with him [are] called, and chosen, and faithful.

Law-giver Isaiah 33:22 For the LORD [is] our judge, the LORD [is] our lawgiver, the LORD [is] our king; he will save us.

Lamb Revelation 5:6 And I beheld, and, lo, in the midst of the throne and of the four beasts, and in the midst of the elders, stood a Lamb as it had been slain, having seven horns and seven eyes, which are the seven Spirits of God sent forth into all the earth.

Revelation 5:12 Saying with a loud voice, Worthy is the Lamb that was slain to receive power, and riches, and wisdom, and strength, and honour, and glory, and blessing.

Revelation 13:8 And all that dwell upon the earth shall worship him (antichrist), whose names are not written in the book of life of the Lamb slain from the foundation of the world.

Lamb of God John 1:29 The next day John seeth Jesus coming unto him, and saith, Behold the Lamb of God, which taketh away the sin of the world.

John 1:36 And looking upon Jesus as he walked, he saith, Behold the Lamb of God!

Last Adam 1 Corinthians 15:45 And so it is written, The first man Adam was made a living soul; the last Adam [was made] a quickening spirit.

Leader Isaiah 55:4 Behold, I have given him [for] a witness to the people, a leader and commander to the people.

Life John 14:6 Jesus saith unto him, I am the way, the truth, and the life: no man cometh unto the Father, but by me.

Colossians 3:4 When Christ, [who is] our life, shall appear, then shall ye also appear with him in glory.

1 John 1:2 (For the life was manifested, and we have seen [it], and bear witness, and shew unto you that eternal life, which was with the Father, and was manifested unto us;)

Light of the world John 8:12 Then spake Jesus again unto them, saying, I am the light of the world: he that followeth me shall not walk in darkness, but shall have the light of life.

Lion of the tribe of Judah Revelation 5:5 And one of the elders saith unto me, Weep not: behold, the Lion of the tribe of Juda, the Root of David, hath prevailed to open the book, and to loose the seven seals thereof.

Lord of Glory 1 Corinthians 2:8 Which none of the princes of this world knew: for had they known [it], they would not have crucified the Lord of glory.

Lord of all Acts 10:36 The word which [God] sent unto the children of Israel, preaching peace by Jesus Christ: (he is Lord of all:)

Lord our righteousness Jeremiah 23:6 In his days Judah shall be saved, and Israel shall dwell safely: and this [is] his name whereby he shall be called, THE LORD OUR RIGHTEOUSNESS.

Lord God of the holy prophets Revelation 22:6 And he said unto me, These sayings [are] faithful and true: and the Lord God of the holy prophets sent his angel to shew unto his servants the things which must shortly be done.

Lord God Almighty Revelation 15:3 And they sing the song of Moses the servant of God, and the song of the Lamb, saying, Great and marvellous [are] thy works, Lord God Almighty; just and true [are] thy ways, thou King of saints.

Mediator 1 Timothy 2:5 For [there is] one God, and one mediator between God and men, the man Christ Jesus;

Messenger of the covenant Malachi 3:1 Behold, I will send my messenger, and he shall prepare the way before me: and the Lord, whom ye seek, shall suddenly come to his temple, even the messenger of the covenant, whom ye delight in: behold, he shall come, saith the LORD of hosts.

Messiah Daniel 9:25 Know therefore and understand, [that] from the going forth of the commandment to restore and to build Jerusalem unto the Messiah the Prince [shall be] seven weeks, and threescore and two weeks: the street shall be built again, and the wall, even in troublous times.

John 1:41 He first findeth his own brother Simon, and saith unto him, We have found the Messias, which is, being interpreted, the Christ.

Mighty God Isaiah 9:6 For unto us a child is born, unto us a son is given: and the government shall be upon his shoulder: and his name shall be called Wonderful, Counsellor, The mighty God, The everlasting Father, The Prince of Peace.

Mighty One of Jacob Isaiah 60:16b and thou shalt know that I the LORD [am] thy Saviour and thy Redeemer, the mighty One of Jacob.

Morning Star Revelation 22:16 I Jesus have sent mine angel to testify unto you these things in the churches. I am the root and the offspring of David, [and] the bright and morning star.

Nazarene Matthew 2:23 And he came and dwelt in a city called Nazareth: that it might be fulfilled which was spoken by the prophets, He shall be called a Nazarene.

Offspring of David Revelation 22:16 I Jesus have sent mine angel to testify unto you these things in the churches. I am the root and the offspring of David, [and] the bright and morning star.

Only begotten John 1:14 And the Word was made flesh, and dwelt among us, (and we beheld his glory, the glory as of the only begotten of the Father,) full of grace and truth.

Our Passover 1 Corinthians 5:7 Purge out therefore the old leaven, that ye may be a new lump, as ye are unleavened. For even Christ our passover is sacrificed for us:

Plant of renown Ezekiel 34:29 And I will raise up for them a plant of renown, and they shall be no more consumed with hunger in the land, neither bear the shame of the heathen any more.

Prince of Life Acts 3:15 And killed the Prince of life, whom God hath raised from the dead; whereof we are witnesses.

Prince of Peace Isaiah 9:6 For unto us a child is born, unto us a son is given: and the government shall be upon his shoulder: and his name shall be called Wonderful, Counsellor, The mighty God, The everlasting Father, The Prince of Peace.

Prince of the kings of the earth Revelation 1:5 And from Jesus Christ, [who is] the faithful witness, [and] the first begotten of the dead, and the prince of the kings of the earth. Unto him that loved us, and washed us from our sins in his own blood,

Prophet Luke 24:19 And he said unto them, What things? And they said unto him, Concerning Jesus of Nazareth, which was a prophet mighty in deed and word before God and all the people:

John 7:40 Many of the people therefore, when they heard this saying, said, Of a truth this is the Prophet.

Ransom 1 Timothy 2:6 Who gave himself a ransom for all, to be testified in due time.

Redeemer Job 19:25 For I know [that] my redeemer liveth, and [that] he shall stand at the latter [day] upon the earth:

Isaiah 59:20 And the Redeemer shall come to Zion, and unto them that turn from transgression in Jacob, saith the LORD.

60:16b : and thou shalt know that I the LORD [am] thy Saviour and thy Redeemer, the mighty One of Jacob.

Resurrection and Life John 11:25 Jesus said unto her, I am the resurrection, and the life: he that believeth in me, though he were dead, yet shall he live:

Rock 1 Corinthians 10:4 And did all drink the same spiritual drink: for they drank of that spiritual Rock that followed them: and that Rock was Christ.

Root of David Revelation 22:16 I Jesus have sent mine angel to testify unto you these things in the churches. I am the root and the offspring of David, [and] the bright and morning star.

Root of Jesse Isaiah 11:10 And in that day there shall be a root of Jesse, which shall stand for an ensign of the people; to it shall the Gentiles seek: and his rest shall be glorious.

Ruler of Israel Micah 5:2 But thou, Bethlehem Ephratah, [though] thou be little among the thousands of Judah, [yet] out of thee shall he come forth unto me [that is] to be ruler in Israel; whose goings forth [have been] from of old, from everlasting.

Savior 2 Peter 2:20 For if after they have escaped the pollutions of the world through the knowledge of the Lord and Saviour Jesus Christ, they are again entangled therein, and overcome, the latter end is worse with them than the beginning.

2 Peter 3:18 But grow in grace, and [in] the knowledge of our Lord and Saviour Jesus Christ. To him [be] glory both now and for ever. Amen.

Servant Isaiah 42:1 Behold my servant, whom I uphold; mine elect, [in whom] my soul delighteth; I have put my spirit upon him: he shall bring forth judgment to the Gentiles.

Isaiah 52:13 Behold, my servant shall deal prudently, he shall be exalted and extolled, and be very high.

Shepherd and Bishop of souls 1 Peter 2:25 For ye were as sheep going astray; but are now returned unto the Shepherd and Bishop of your souls.

Shiloh Genesis 49:10 The sceptre shall not depart from Judah, nor a lawgiver from between his feet, until Shiloh come; and unto him [shall] the gathering of the people [be].

Son of the blessed Mark 14:61 But he held his peace, and answered nothing. Again the high priest asked him, and said unto him, Art thou the Christ, the Son of the Blessed?

Son of God Luke 1:35 And the angel answered and said unto her, The Holy Ghost shall come upon thee, and the power of the Highest shall overshadow thee: therefore also that holy thing which shall be born of thee shall be called the Son of God.

John 1:49 Nathanael answered and saith unto him, Rabbi, thou art the Son of God; thou art the King of Israel.

Son of the Highest Luke 1:32 He shall be great, and shall be called the Son of the Highest: and the Lord God shall give unto him the throne of his father David:

Son of David Matthew 9:27 And when Jesus departed thence, two blind men followed him, crying, and saying, [Thou] Son of David, have mercy on us.

Son of man John 5:27 And hath given him authority to execute judgment also, because he is the Son of man.

Star Numbers 24:17 I shall see him, but not now: I shall behold him, but not nigh: there shall come a Star out of Jacob, and a Sceptre shall rise out of Israel, and shall smite the corners of Moab, and destroy all the children of Sheth.

Sun of righteousness Malachi 4:2 But unto you that fear my name shall the Sun of righteousness arise with healing in his wings; and ye shall go forth, and grow up as calves of the stall.

Surety Hebrews 7:22 By so much was Jesus made a surety of a better testament.

True God 1 John 5:20 And we know that the Son of God is come, and hath given us an understanding, that we may know him that is true, and we are in him that is true, [even] in his Son Jesus Christ. This is the true God, and eternal life.

True Light John 1:9 [That] was the true Light, which lighteth every man that cometh into the world.

True Vine John 15:1 I am the true vine, and my Father is the husbandman.

Truth John 14:6 Jesus saith unto him, I am the way, the truth, and the life: no man cometh unto the Father, but by me.

Way John 14:6 Jesus saith unto him, I am the way, the truth, and the life: no man cometh unto the Father, but by me.

Wisdom Proverbs 8:12 I wisdom dwell with prudence, and find out knowledge of witty inventions.

Witness Isaiah 55:4 Behold, I have given him [for] a witness to the people, a leader and commander to the people.

Wonderful Isaiah 9:6 For unto us a child is born, unto us a son is given: and the government shall be upon his shoulder: and his name shall be called Wonderful, Counsellor, The mighty God, The everlasting Father, The Prince of Peace.

Word John 1:1 In the beginning was the Word, and the Word was with God, and the Word was God.

1 John 5:7 For there are three that bear record in heaven, the Father, the Word, and the Holy Ghost: and these three are one.

Word of God Revelation 19:13 And he [was] clothed with a vesture dipped in blood: and his name is called The Word of God.

Word of Life 1 John 1:1 That which was from the beginning, which we have heard, which we have seen with our eyes, which we have looked upon, and our hands have handled, of the Word of life;

CHAPTER 10

WHAT GOD SAYS ABOUT LOVE

Make the following prayer personal:

Ephesians 3:16 May He grant you out of the rich treasury of His glory to be strengthened and reinforced with mighty power in the inner man by the Holy Spirit Himself - indwelling your innermost being and personality.

Ephesians 3:17 May Christ through your faith actually dwell, settle down, abide, make His permanent home in your hearts! May you be rooted deep in love and founded securely on love,

Ephesians 3:18 So that you may have the power and be strong to apprehend and grasp with all the saints (God's devoted people) the experience of that love, what is the breadth and length and height and depth of it,

Ephesians 3:19 That you may really come to know - practically, through experience for yourselves - the love of Christ, which far surpasses mere knowledge without experience, that you may be filled through all your being unto all the fullness of God - [that is] that you may have the richest measure of the Divine Presence, and become a body wholly filled and flooded with God Himself!

Matthew 5:44 But I say unto you, love your enemies, bless them that curse you, do good to them that hurt you, and pray for them which despitefully use you, and persecute you.

Matthew 5:5 Blessed are the meek: for they shall inherit the earth.

[Meek = teachable, humble in spirit, lowly of mind, not proud, gentle, kind, slow to take or give offense, self-controlled, strength grown tender, considerate, courteous, never inflicts wounds, lightens the load.]

Matthew 5:7 Blessed are the merciful; for they shall obtain mercy.

Matthew 7:12 Do unto others as you would have others do unto you.

John 13:34 A new commandment I give unto you, That you love one another; as I have loved you, that you also love one another.

John 13:35 By this shall all men know that you are my disciples, if you have love one to another.

Romans 5:5 The love of God is shed abroad in our hearts by the Holy Ghost.

(The love of God and the compassion of Jesus has been poured out within our hearts through the Holy Spirit who has been given unto us.)

Romans 12:9-21 Let your love be sincere, without hypocrisy. Abhor that which is evil; cling and cleave to that which is good.

12:10 Be kindly affectioned and devoted one to another with brotherly love; in honor preferring (give preference to) one another.

12:11 not lagging behind, (slothful) in diligence, zeal, earnest endeavor; be aglow and burning with the Spirit serving the Lord.

12:12 Rejoicing in hope, patient (constant) in tribulation; be constantly devoted to prayer.

12:13 Distributing (giving) to the needs of the saints; practicing hospitality.

12:14 Bless them who persecute you; bless and curse not.

12:15 Share others' joy, rejoicing with those who rejoice; and share other' grief, weeping with those who weep.

12:16 Be of the same mind (live in harmony) with one another. Do not be haughty, snobbish, high-minded, exclusive, but readily adjust yourself to people and things and give yourselves to humble tasks. Never over-estimate yourself or be wise in your own conceits.

12:17 Recompense to no man evil for evil, but take thought for what is honest and proper and noble - aiming to be above reproach - in the sight of everyone.

12:18 If possible, as far as it depends on you, live at peace with everyone.

Romans 12:19 Beloved, never avenge yourselves, but leave the way open for God's wrath: for it is written, Vengeance is Mine, I will repay, says the Lord.

Romans 12:20 Therefore, if thine enemy hunger, feed him; if he thirsts, give him drink: for in so doing thou shalt heap coals of fire on his head.

Romans 12:21 Be not overcome of evil, but overcome evil with good.

1 Peter 4:8 And above all things have fervent charity (intense and unfailing love) among yourselves: for charity shall cover the multitude of sins.

1 John 2:5 But whoso keeps His word, in him verily is the love of God perfected: hereby we know that we are in Him.

1 John 2:10 He that loves his brother abides in the light, and there is none occasion of stumbling in him.

1 John 3:16 Hereby we perceive the love of God, because he laid down His life for us: and we ought to lay down our lives for the brethren.

1 John 3:17 But whoso has this world's goods, and sees his brother have need, and shuts up his bowels (heart) of compassion from him, how dwelleth the love of God in him?

1 John 3:18 My little children, let us not love merely in word or in tongue; but in deed and in truth - in practice and sincerity.

1 John 4:7 Beloved, let us love one another: for love is of God; and every one that loveth is born of God, and knoweth God.

1 John 4:8 He that loveth not, knoweth not God; for God is love.

1 John 4:9 In this was manifested the love of God toward us, because that God sent His only begotten Son into the world, that we might live through Him.

1 John 4:10 Herein is love, not that we loved God, but that He loved us, and sent His Son to be the propitiation (the atoning sacrifice) for our sins.

1 John 4:11 Beloved, if God so loved us, we ought also to love one another.

1 John 4:12 No man has seen God at any time. If we love one another, God dwells in us, and his love is perfected in us.

1 John 4:13 Hereby we know that we dwell in Him, and He in us, because He has given us of His Spirit.

1 John 4:14 And we have seen and do testify that the Father sent the Son to be the Savior of the world.

1 John 4:15 Whosoever shall confess that Jesus is the Son of God, God dwells in him, and he in God.

1 John 4:16 And we have known and believed the love that God has to us. God is love: and he that dwells in love dwells in God, and God dwells in him.

1 John 4:17 Herein is our love made perfect; so that we may have boldness in the day of judgment: because as He is, so are we in this world.

1 John 4:18 There is no fear in love: but perfect love casts out fear: because fear has torment. He that fears is not made perfect in love.

1 John 4:19 We love Him because He first loved us.

1 John 4:20 If a man say, "I love God," and hates his brother he is a liar: for he that loves not his brother whom he has seen, how can he love God whom he has not seen?

1 John 4:21 And this commandment we have from Him: that he who loves God love his brother also.

Jude 21 Guard and keep yourselves in the love of God.

Matthew 18:27 Then the lord of that servant was moved with compassion, and loosed him, and forgave him the debt.

1 Corinthians 8:1 Charity edifies. (Love, affection, goodwill, benevolence edifies and builds up and encourages one to grow to his full stature.)

1 Corinthians 13:4 Love endures long and is patient and kind; love is never envious nor boils over with jealousy; is not boastful or vainglorious, does not display itself haughtily.

1 Corinthians 13:5 It is not conceited - arrogant and inflated with pride; it is not rude (unmannerly), and does not act unbecomingly. Love (God's love in us) does not insist on its own rights or its own way, for it is not self-seeking; it is not touchy or fretful or resentful; it takes no account of the evil done to it - pays no attention to a suffered wrong.

1 Corinthians 13:6 It does not rejoice at injustice and unrighteousness, but rejoices when right and truth prevail.

1 Corinthians 13:7 Love bears up under anything and everything that comes, is ever ready to believe the best of every person, its hopes are fadeless under all circumstances and it endures everything without weakening.

1 Corinthians 13:8 Love never fails - never fades out or becomes obsolete or comes to an end.

1 Corinthians 13:13 Love is true affection for God and man, growing out of God's love for and in us.

1 Corinthians 14:1 Eagerly pursue and seek to acquire this love - make it your aim, your great quest.

Colossians 3:14 And above all these things put on love, which is the bond of perfectness (the perfect bond of unity).

Romans 13:8 We must owe love to one another: for he that loves another has fulfilled the law.

Romans 13:9 Thou shalt love thy neighbor as thyself.

Romans 13:10 Love does no wrong to one's neighbor - it never hurts anybody. Therefore love meets all the requirements and is the fulfilling of the law.

2 Corinthians 5:14 For the love of Christ constrains, controls, urges and impels us.

Galatians 5:6 Faith works by love (through love).

Galatians 5:13 By love serve one another.

Galatians 5:22 The fruit of the Spirit is love...

Ephesians 4:2 With all lowliness (humility) and meekness, with longsuffering, forbearing one another in love.

Ephesians 4:15 But speaking the truth in love...

Ephesians 5:2 Walk in love...

Philippians 1:9 And this I pray, that your love may abound yet more and more in knowledge and in all judgment.

1 Thessalonians 3:12 And the Lord make you to increase and abound, excel, and overflow in love one toward another, and toward all men, even as we do toward you:

1 Thessalonians 3:13 To the end (so that) He may establish your hearts unblameable in holiness (and faultlessly pure) before God...

1 Thessalonians 4:9 But as touching [regarding] brotherly love you need not that I write unto you: for you yourselves are taught of God to love one another.

1 Thessalonians 5:8 Put on the breastplate of faith and love...

2 Timothy 1:7 For God did not give us a spirit of timidity - of cowardice, of craven and cringing and fawning fear - but He has given us a Spirit of power and of love and of calm and well-balanced mind and discipline and self-control.

1 Peter 1:22 Seeing you have purified your souls in obeying the truth through the Spirit unto unfeigned (sincere) love of the brethren, see that you love one another with a pure heart fervently.

1 Peter 3:8 Finally, be ye all of one mind, having compassion one of another, love as brethren, be pitiful (kindhearted), be courteous.

Romans 12:9 Let your love be sincere - a real thing, without hypocrisy; hate what is evil (loath all ungodliness, turn in horror from wickedness), but hold fast to that which is good.

Romans 12:10 Be devoted to and love one another with brotherly love and affection - as members of one family - giving precedence and showing honor to one another.

Romans 12:11 Never lag in zeal and in earnest endeavor; be aglow and burning with the Spirit, serving the Lord.
Romans 12:12 Rejoice and exult in hope; be steadfast and patient in suffering and tribulation; be constant in and devoted to prayer.
Romans 12:13 Contribute to the needs of God's people - sharing in the necessities of the saints - pursuing the practice of hospitality.

CHAPTER 11

THE KINGDOM IN REVELATION AND DANIEL

1 Corinthians 15:23 But each in his own rank and turn: Christ the Messiah is the firstfruits, then those who are Christ's own will be resurrected at His coming.
1 Corinthians 15:24 After that comes the end (the completion), when He delivers over the kingdom to God the Father after rendering inoperative and abolishing every [other] rule and every authority and power.
Revelation 10:5 Then the mighty angel whom I had seen stationed on sea and land raised his right hand to heaven (the sky),
Daniel 12:6 And one said to the man clothed in linen, who was above the waters of the river, How long shall it be to the end of these wonders?
Daniel 12:7 And I heard the man clothed in linen, who was above the waters of the river, when he held up his right and his left hand toward the heavens and swore by Him Who lives forever that it shall be for a time, times, and a half a time [or three and one-half years]; and when they have made an end of shattering and crushing the power of the holy people, all these things shall be finished.
Revelation 10:6 And swore in the name of (by) Him Who lives forever and ever, Who created the heavens and all they contain, and the earth and all that it contains, and the sea and all that it contains. He swore that no more time should intervene and there should be no more waiting or delay,
Revelation 10:7 But that when the days come when the trumpet call of the seventh angel is about to be sounded, then God's mystery (His secret design, His hidden purpose), as He had announced the glad tidings to His servants the prophets, should be fulfilled (accomplished, completed).

Revelation 11:15 The seventh angel then blew his trumpet, and there were mighty voices in heaven, shouting, The dominion (kingdom, sovereignty, rule) of the world has now come into the possession and become the kingdom of our Lord and of His Christ (the Messiah), and He shall reign forever and ever (for the eternities of the eternities)!
Daniel 7.13 I saw in the night visions, and behold, on the clouds of the heavens came One like a Son of man, and He came to the Ancient of Days and was presented before Him.
Daniel 7:14 And there was given Him [the Messiah] dominion and glory and kingdom, that all peoples, nations, and languages should serve Him. His dominion is an everlasting dominion which shall not pass away, and His kingdom is one which shall not be destroyed.
Daniel 7:27 And the kingdom and the dominion and the greatness of the kingdom under the whole heavens shall be given to the people of the saints of the Most High; His kingdom is an everlasting kingdom, and all the dominions shall serve and obey Him.

Revelation 11:16 Then the twenty-four elders of the heavenly Sanhedrin, who sit on their thrones before God, prostrated themselves before Him and worshiped,

Revelation 11:17 Exclaiming, To You we give thanks, Lord God Omnipotent, the One Who is and ever was, for assuming the high sovereignty and the great power that are Yours and for beginning to reign.

Revelation 11:18 And the heathen (the nations) raged, but Your wrath (retribution, indignation) came, the time when the dead will be judged and Your servants the prophets and saints rewarded—and those who revere (fear) Your name, both low and high and small and great—and the time for destroying the corrupters of the earth.

Psalms 2:1 Why do the nations assemble with commotion [uproar and confusion of voices], and why do the people imagine (meditate upon and devise) an empty scheme?

Daniel 7:13 I saw in the night visions, and behold, on the clouds of the heavens came One like a Son of man, and He came to the Ancient of Days and was presented before Him.

Daniel 7:14 And there was given Him [the Messiah] dominion and glory and kingdom, that all peoples, nations, and languages should serve Him. His dominion is an everlasting dominion which shall not pass away, and His kingdom is one which shall not be destroyed.

Revelation 5:1 And I saw lying on the open hand of Him Who was seated on the throne a scroll (book) written within and on the back, closed and sealed with seven seals;

Revelation 5:2 And I saw a strong angel announcing in a loud voice, Who is worthy to open the scroll? And [who is entitled and deserves and is morally fit] to break its seals?

Revelation 5:3 And no one in heaven or on earth or under the earth [in the realm of the dead, Hades] was able to open the scroll or to take a [single] look at its contents.

Revelation 5:4 And I wept audibly and bitterly because no one was found fit to open the scroll or to inspect it.

Revelation 5:5 Then one of the elders of the heavenly Sanhedrin] said to me, Stop weeping! See, the Lion of the tribe of Judah, the Root (Source) of David, has won (has overcome and conquered)! He can open the scroll and break its seven seals!

Revelation 5:6 And there between the throne and the four living creatures (beings) and among the elders of the heavenly Sanhedrin I saw a Lamb standing, as though it had been slain, with seven horns and with seven eyes, which are the seven Spirits of God [the sevenfold Holy Spirit] Who have been sent [on duty far and wide] into all the earth.

Revelation 5:7 He then went and took the scroll from the right hand of Him Who sat on the throne.

Revelation 5:8 And when He had taken the scroll, the four living creatures and the twenty-four elders of the heavenly Sanhedrin prostrated themselves before the Lamb. Each was holding a harp (lute or guitar), and they had golden bowls full of incense (fragrant spices and gums for burning), which are the prayers of God's people (the saints).

Revelation 5:9 And [now] they sing a new song, saying, You are worthy to take the scroll and to break the seals that are on it, for You were slain (sacrificed), and with Your blood You purchased men unto God from every tribe and language and people and nation.

Revelation 5:10 And You have made them a kingdom (royal race) and priests to our God, and they shall reign [as kings] over the earth!

Daniel 7:18 But the saints of the Most High [God] shall receive the kingdom and possess the kingdom forever, even forever and ever.

Romans 8.17 And if we are [His] children, then we are [His] heirs also: heirs of God and fellow heirs with Christ [sharing His inheritance with Him]; only we must share His suffering if we are to share His glory.

1 Peter 2.9 But you are a chosen race, a royal priesthood, a dedicated nation, [God's] own purchased, special people, that you may set forth the wonderful deeds and display the virtues and perfections of Him Who called you out of darkness into His marvelous light.

Revelation 3.21 He who overcomes (is victorious), I will grant him to sit beside Me on My throne, as I Myself overcame (was victorious) and sat down beside My Father on His throne.

Daniel 7:21 As I looked, this horn made war with the saints and prevailed over them

Revelation 13:7 He was further permitted to wage war on God's holy people (the saints) and to overcome them. And power was given him to extend his authority over every tribe and people and tongue and nation,

Revelation 13:8 And all the inhabitants of the earth will fall down in adoration and pay him homage, everyone whose name has not been recorded in the Book of Life of the Lamb that was slain [in sacrifice] from the foundation of the world.

Revelation 13:9 If anyone is able to hear, let him listen:

Daniel 7:22 Until the Ancient of Days came, and judgment was given to the saints of the Most High [God], and the time came when the saints possessed the kingdom.

Daniel 7:27 And the kingdom and the dominion and the greatness of the kingdom under the whole heavens shall be given to the people of the saints of the Most High; His kingdom is an everlasting kingdom, and all the dominions shall serve and obey Him.

1 Thessalonians 4:13 Now also we would not have you ignorant, brethren, about those who fall asleep in death], that you may not grieve [for them] as the rest do who have no hope [beyond the grave].

1 Thessalonians 4:14 For since we believe that Jesus died and rose again, even so God will also bring with Him through Jesus those who have fallen asleep in death].

1 Thessalonians 4:15 For this we declare to you by the Lord's [own] word, that we who are alive and remain until the coming of the Lord shall in no way precede [into His presence] or have any advantage at all over those who have previously fallen asleep [in Him in death].

1 Thessalonians 4:16 For the Lord Himself will descend from heaven with a loud cry of summons, with the shout of an archangel, and with the blast of the trumpet of God. And those who have departed this life in Christ will rise first.

1 Thessalonians 4:17 Then we, the living ones who remain [on the earth], shall simultaneously be caught up along with [the resurrected dead] in the clouds to meet the Lord in the air; and so always (through the eternity of the eternities) we shall be with the Lord!

1 Corinthians 15:51 Behold, I shew you a mystery; We shall not all sleep, but we shall all be changed,

1 Corinthians 15:52 In a moment, in the twinkling of an eye, at the last trump: for the trumpet shall sound, and the dead shall be raised incorruptible, and we shall be changed.

CHAPTER 12

OVERCOMING FEAR

Fear takes on many forms. There are hundreds of phobias. Don't allow yourself to be in bondage any longer to your fears. God loves you. Study and meditate on the Bible scriptures below to help you overcome all your fears.

Job 3:25 For the thing which I greatly feared is come upon me, and that which I was afraid of is come unto me.
Job 5:21 Thou shalt be hid from the scourge of the tongue: neither shalt thou be afraid of destruction when it cometh.
Job 5:22 At destruction and famine thou shalt laugh: neither shalt thou be afraid of the beasts of the earth.
Job 11:9 Also thou shalt lie down, and none shall make [thee] afraid; yea, many shall make suit unto thee.

Psalms 3:6 I will not be afraid of ten thousands of people, that have set themselves against me round about.
Psalms 27:1 The LORD is my light and my salvation; whom shall I fear? the LORD is the strength of my life; of whom shall I be afraid?
Psalms 56:3 What time I am afraid, I will trust in thee.
Psalms 56:11 In God have I put my trust: I will not be afraid what man can do unto me.
Psalms 91:5 Thou shalt not be afraid for the terror by night; nor for the arrow that flieth by day;
Psalms 112:7 He shall not be afraid of evil tidings: his heart is fixed, trusting in the LORD.
Psalms 112:8 His heart is established, he shall not be afraid, until he see his desire upon his enemies.

Proverbs 3:24 When thou liest down, thou shalt not be afraid: yea, thou shalt lie down, and thy sleep shall be sweet.
Proverbs 3:25 Be not afraid of sudden fear, neither of the desolation of the wicked, when it cometh.

Isaiah 12:2 Behold, God is my salvation; I will trust, and not be afraid: for the LORD JEHOVAH is my strength and my song; he also is become my salvation.

Isaiah 44:8 Fear ye not, neither be afraid: have not I told thee from that time, and have declared it? ye are even my witnesses. Is there a God beside me? yea, there is no God; I know not any.

Matthew 17:7 And Jesus came and touched them, and said, Arise, and be not afraid.

Mark 5:36 As soon as Jesus heard the word that was spoken, he saith unto the ruler of the synagogue, Be not afraid, only believe.

John 14:27 Peace I leave with you, my peace I give unto you: not as the world giveth, give I unto you. Let not your heart be troubled, neither let it be afraid.

Psalms 23:4 Yea, though I walk through the valley of the shadow of death, I will fear no evil: for thou art with me; thy rod and thy staff they comfort me.
Psalms 27:3 Though an host should encamp against me, my heart shall not fear: though war should rise against me, in this will I be confident.
Psalms 64:1 Hear my voice, O God, in my prayer: preserve my life from fear of the enemy.
Psalms 118:6 The LORD is on my side; I will not fear: what can man do unto me?

Proverbs 1:33 But whoso hearkeneth unto me shall dwell safely, and shall be quiet from fear of evil.
Proverbs 3:25 Be not afraid of sudden fear, neither of the desolation of the wicked, when it cometh.
Proverbs 29:25 The fear of man bringeth a snare: but whoso putteth his trust in the LORD shall be safe.

Isaiah 41:10 Fear thou not; for I am with thee: be not dismayed; for I am thy God: I will strengthen thee; yea, I will help thee; yea, I will uphold thee with the right hand of my righteousness.
Isaiah 41:13 For I the LORD thy God will hold thy right hand, saying unto thee, Fear not; I will help thee.
Isaiah 43:1 But now thus saith the LORD that created thee, O Jacob, and he that formed thee, O Israel, Fear not: for I have redeemed thee, I have called thee by thy name; thou art mine.
Isaiah 43:5 Fear not: for I am with thee: I will bring thy seed from the east, and gather thee from the west;
Isaiah 54:4 Fear not; for thou shalt not be ashamed: neither be thou confounded; for thou shalt not be put to shame: for thou shalt forget the shame of thy youth, and shalt not remember the reproach of thy widowhood any more.
Isaiah 54:14 In righteousness shalt thou be established: thou shalt be far from oppression; for thou shalt not fear: and from terror; for it shall not come near thee.

Luke 21:26 Men's hearts failing them for fear, and for looking after those things which are coming on the earth: for the powers of heaven shall be shaken.

2 Timothy 1:7 For God hath not given us the spirit of fear; but of power, and of love, and of a sound mind.

1 John 4:18 There is no fear in love; but perfect love casteth out fear: because fear hath torment. He that feareth is not made perfect in love.

Isaiah 35:4 Say to them that are of a fearful heart, Be strong, fear not: behold, your God will come with vengeance, even God with a recompence; he will come and save you.

Matthew 8:26 And he saith unto them, Why are ye fearful, O ye of little faith? Then he arose, and rebuked the winds and the sea; and there was a great calm.

Mark 4:40 And he said unto them, Why are ye so fearful? how is it that ye have no faith?

Revelation 21:8 But the fearful, and unbelieving, and the abominable, and murderers, and whoremongers, and sorcerers, and idolaters, and all liars, shall have their part in the lake which burneth with fire and brimstone: which is the second death.

Psalms 34:4 I sought the LORD, and he heard me, and delivered me from all my fears.

CHAPTER 13

VERSES WHERE OUR HEAVENLY FATHER IS MENTIONED

Matthew 5.16 Let your light so shine before men, that they may see your good works, and glorify your Father which is in heaven.

Matthew 5:45 That ye may be the children of your Father which is in heaven: for he maketh his sun to rise on the evil and on the good, and sendeth rain on the just and on the unjust.

Matthew 5.48 Be ye therefore perfect, even as your Father which is in heaven is perfect.

Matthew 6.1 Take heed that ye do not your alms before men, to be seen of them: otherwise ye have no reward of your Father which is in heaven.

Matthew 6.4 That thine alms may be in secret: and thy Father which seeth in secret himself shall reward thee openly. **(When I give in secret my Father will reward me openly.)**

Matthew 6.6 But thou, when thou prayest, enter into thy closet, and when thou hast shut thy door, pray to thy Father which is in secret; and thy Father which seeth in secret shall reward thee openly. **(When I pray in secret my Father will reward me openly.)**

Matthew 6.8 Be not ye therefore like unto them: for your Father knoweth what things ye have need of, before ye ask him.

Matthew 6.9 After this manner therefore pray ye: Our Father which art in heaven, Hallowed be thy name. **(My Father knows what I need before I ask Him.)**

Matthew 6.14 For if ye forgive men their trespasses, your heavenly Father will also forgive you:

Matthew 6.15 But if ye forgive not men their trespasses, neither will your Father forgive your trespasses. **(I forgive quickly and my Father forgives me.)**

Matthew 6.18 That thou appear not unto men to fast, but unto thy Father which is in secret: and thy Father, which seeth in secret, shall reward thee openly. **(When I fast in secret my Father will reward me openly.)**

Matthew 6.26 Behold the fowls of the air: for they sow not, neither do they reap, nor gather into barns; yet your heavenly Father feedeth them. Are ye not much better than they? **(My Father feeds the animals; I'm much better than the animals so my Father will supply all that I need.)**

Matthew 6.32 **(For after all these things do the Gentiles seek:)** for your heavenly Father knoweth that ye have need of all these things.

Matthew 6.33 But seek ye first the kingdom of God, and his righteousness; and all these things shall be added unto you. **(My heavenly Father knows that I have need of all these things, and He supplies my needs abundantly because I seek first His kingdom and righteousness.)**

Matthew 7.11 If ye then, being evil, know how to give good gifts unto your children, how much more shall your Father which is in heaven give good things to them that ask him? **(My Heavenly Father blesses me with good gifts, exceedingly abundantly above all I can ask or think.)**

Matthew 7.21 Not every one that saith unto me, Lord, Lord, shall enter into the kingdom of heaven; but he that doeth the will of my Father which is in heaven. **(I do the will of my Father, not seeking my own will.)**

Matthew 10.20 For it is not ye that speak, but the Spirit of your Father which speaketh in you. **(The Spirit of my Heavenly Father speaks in me.)**

Matthew 10.29 Are not two sparrows sold for a farthing? and one of them shall not fall on the ground without your Father. **(Father is in control, He is on the throne.)**

Matthew 10.32 Whosoever therefore shall confess me before men, him will I confess also before my Father which is in heaven.

Matthew 10.33 But whosoever shall deny me before men, him will I also deny before my Father which is in heaven. **(I boldly confess Jesus before men, and Jesus brags to my Father about me.)**

Matthew 11.25 At that time Jesus answered and said, I thank thee, O Father, Lord of heaven and earth, because thou hast hid these things from the wise and prudent, and hast revealed them unto babes.

Matthew 11.26 Even so, Father: for so it seemed good in thy sight.

Matthew 11.27 All things are delivered unto me of my Father: and no man knoweth the Son, but the Father; neither knoweth any man the Father, save the Son, and [he] to whomsoever the Son will reveal [him]. **(Thank you, my Father, for revealing your secret things unto me daily. Jesus is daily revealing the Father unto me.)**

Matthew 12.50 For whosoever shall do the will of my Father which is in heaven, the same is my brother, and sister, and mother. **(I do the will of my Father, I receive His free love gift of His precious Son Jesus, and I am a brother of Jesus.)**

Matthew 13:43 Then shall the righteous shine forth as the sun in the kingdom of their Father. Who hath ears to hear, let him hear. **(I am righteous and I shine forth in my Father's kingdom.)**

Matthew 15:13 But he answered and said, Every plant, which my heavenly Father hath not planted, shall be rooted up. **(My Father has planted me, I am abiding in the Vine and I am growing spiritually.)**

Matthew 16:17 And Jesus answered and said unto him, Blessed art thou, Simon Barjona: for flesh and blood hath not revealed [it] unto thee, but my Father which is in heaven. **(My father reveals secrets to me.)**

Matthew 16:27 For the Son of man shall come in the glory of his Father with his angels; and then he shall reward every man according to his works. **(My Father will reward me when He comes to earth with Jesus.)**

Matthew 18:10 Take heed that ye despise not one of these little ones; for I say unto you, That in heaven their angels do always behold the face of my Father which is in heaven. **(Children have angels who behold the face of my Father. Thank you Father for You and Your angels protecting my entire family.)**

Matthew 18:14 Even so it is not the will of your Father which is in heaven, that one of these little ones should perish. **(It is not the will of my Father that these little ones perish.)**

Matthew 18:19 Again I say unto you, That if two of you shall agree on earth as touching any thing that they shall ask, it shall be done for them of my Father which is in heaven. **(My Father loves answering my prayers.)**

Matthew 18:35 So likewise shall my heavenly Father do also unto you, if ye from your hearts forgive not every one his brother their trespasses. **(I quickly forgive those who do me wrong.)**

Matthew 20:23 And he saith unto them, Ye shall drink indeed of my cup, and be baptized with the baptism that I am baptized with: but to sit on my right hand, and on my left, is not mine to give, but [it shall be given to them] for whom it is prepared of my Father. **(My Father is preparing a place for me in His Kingdom.)**

Matthew 23:9 And call no [man] your father upon the earth: for one is your Father, which is in heaven.

Matthew 24:36 But of that day and hour knoweth no [man], no, not the angels of heaven, but my Father only. **(Only my Father knows when Jesus will come.)**

Matthew 25:34 Then shall the King say unto them on his right hand, Come, ye blessed of my Father, inherit the kingdom prepared for you from the foundation of the world: **(I'm blessed and I'm inheriting the Kingdom.)**

Matthew 26:29 But I say unto you, I will not drink henceforth of this fruit of the vine, until that day when I drink it new with you in my Father's kingdom.

Matthew 26:39 And he went a little further, and fell on his face, and prayed, saying, O my Father, if it be possible, let this cup pass from me: nevertheless not as I will, but as thou [wilt].

Matthew 26:42 He went away again the second time, and prayed, saying, O my Father, if this cup may not pass away from me, except I drink it, thy will be done.

Matthew 26:53 Thinkest thou that I cannot now pray to my Father, and he shall presently give me more than twelve legions of angels?

Matthew 28:19 Go ye therefore, and teach all nations, baptizing them in the name of the Father, and of the Son, and of the Holy Ghost:

Mark 8.38 Whosoever therefore shall be ashamed of me and of my words in this adulterous and sinful generation; of him also shall the Son of man be ashamed, when he cometh in the glory of his Father with the holy angels.

Mark 11.25 And when ye stand praying, forgive, if ye have ought against any: that your Father also which is in heaven may forgive you your trespasses.

Mark 11.26 But if ye do not forgive, neither will your Father which is in heaven forgive your trespasses.

Mark 13.32 But of that day and [that] hour knoweth no man, no, not the angels which are in heaven, neither the Son, but the Father.

Mark 14.36 And he said, Abba, Father, all things [are] possible unto thee; take away this cup from me: nevertheless not what I will, but what thou wilt.

Luke 2.49 And he said unto them, How is it that ye sought me? wist ye not that I must be about my Father's business?

Luke 6.36 Be ye therefore merciful, as your Father also is merciful.

Luke 9.26 For whosoever shall be ashamed of me and of my words, of him shall the Son of man be ashamed, when he shall come in his own glory, and [in his] Father's, and of the holy angels.

Luke 10.21 In that hour Jesus rejoiced in spirit, and said, I thank thee, O Father, Lord of heaven and earth, that thou hast hid these things from the wise and prudent, and hast revealed them unto babes: even so, Father; for so it seemed good in thy sight.

Luke 10.22 All things are delivered to me of my Father: and no man knoweth who the Son is, but the Father; and who the Father is, but the Son, and [he] to whom the Son will reveal [him].

Luke 11.2 And he said unto them, When ye pray, say, Our Father which art in heaven, Hallowed be thy name. Thy kingdom come. Thy will be done, as in heaven, so in earth.

Luke 11.13 If ye then, being evil, know how to give good gifts unto your children: how much more shall [your] heavenly Father give the Holy Spirit to them that ask him?

Luke 12.30 For all these things do the nations of the world seek after: and your Father knoweth that ye have need of these things.

Luke 12.32 Fear not, little flock; for it is your Father's good pleasure to give you the kingdom. **(It is my Father's good pleasure to give me the kingdom.)**

Luke 22.29 And I appoint unto you a kingdom, as my Father hath appointed unto me;

Luke 22.42 Saying, Father, if thou be willing, remove this cup from me: nevertheless not my will, but thine, be done.

Luke 23.34 Then said Jesus, Father, forgive them; for they know not what they do. And they parted his raiment and cast lots.

Luke 23.46 And when Jesus had cried with a loud voice, he said, Father, into thy hands I commend my spirit: and having said thus, he gave up the ghost.

Luke 24.49 And, behold, I send the promise of my Father upon you: but tarry ye in the city of Jerusalem, until ye be endued with power from on high.

John 1.14 And the Word was made flesh, and dwelt among us, and we beheld his glory, the glory as of the only begotten of the Father, full of grace and truth. **(They beheld his glory on the mount of transfiguration.)**

John 1.18 No man hath seen God at any time; the only begotten Son, which is in the bosom of the Father, he hath declared [him].

John 2.16 And said unto them that sold doves, Take these things hence; make not my Father's house an house of merchandise.

John 3.35 The Father loveth the Son, and hath given all things into his hand.

John 4.21 Jesus saith unto her, Woman, believe me, the hour cometh, when ye shall neither in this mountain, nor yet at Jerusalem, worship the Father.

John 4.23 But the hour cometh, and now is, when the true worshippers shall worship the Father in spirit and in truth: for the Father seeketh such to worship him. **(My heavenly Father is seeking me to worship him.)**

John 5.17 But Jesus answered them, My <u>Father</u> worketh hitherto, and I work.

John 5.18 Therefore the Jews sought the more to kill him, because he not only had broken the sabbath, but said also that God was his <u>Father</u>, making himself equal with God.

John 5.19 Then answered Jesus and said unto them, Verily, verily, I say unto you, The Son can do nothing of himself, but what he seeth the <u>Father</u> do: for what things soever he doeth, these also doeth the Son likewise.

John 5.20 For the <u>Father</u> loveth the Son, and sheweth him all things that himself doeth: and he will shew him greater works than these, that ye may marvel.

John 5.21 For as the <u>Father</u> raiseth up the dead, and quickeneth [them]; even so the Son quickeneth whom he will.

John 5.22 For the <u>Father</u> judgeth no man, but hath committed all judgment unto the Son:

John 5.23 That all [men] should honour the Son, even as they honour the <u>Father</u>. He that honoureth not the Son honoureth not the <u>Father</u> which hath sent him.

John 5.26 For as the <u>Father</u> hath life in himself; so hath he given to the Son to have life in himself;

John 5.30 I can of mine own self do nothing: as I hear, I judge: and my judgment is just; because I seek not mine own will, but the will of the <u>Father</u> which hath sent me.

John 5.36 But I have greater witness than [that] of John: for the works which the <u>Father</u> hath given me to finish, the same works that I do, bear witness of me, that the <u>Father</u> hath sent me.

John 5.37 And the <u>Father</u> himself, which hath sent me, hath borne witness of me. Ye have neither heard his voice at any time, nor seen his shape.

John 5.43 I am come in my <u>Father's</u> name, and ye receive me not: if another shall come in his own name, him ye will receive.

John 5.45 Do not think that I will accuse you to the <u>Father</u>: there is [one] that accuseth you, [even] Moses, in whom ye trust.

John 6.27 Labour not for the meat which perisheth, but for that meat which endureth unto everlasting life, which the Son of man shall give unto you: for him hath God the <u>Father</u> sealed.

John 6.32 Then Jesus said unto them, Verily, verily, I say unto you, Moses gave you not that bread from heaven; but my <u>Father</u> giveth you the true bread from heaven.

John 6.37 All that the <u>Father</u> giveth me shall come to me; and him that cometh to me I will in no wise cast out.

John 6.39 And this is the <u>Father's</u> will which hath sent me, that of all which he hath given me I should lose nothing, but should raise it up again at the last day.

John 6.44 No man can come to me, except the <u>Father</u> which hath sent me draw him: and I will raise him up at the last day.

John 6.45 It is written in the prophets, And they shall be all taught of God. Every man therefore that hath heard, and hath learned of the <u>Father</u>, cometh unto me.

John 6.46 Not that any man hath seen the <u>Father</u>, save he which is of God, he hath seen the <u>Father</u>.

John 6.57 As the living <u>Father</u> hath sent me, and I live by the <u>Father</u>: so he that eateth me, even he shall live by me.

John 6.65 And he said, Therefore said I unto you, that no man can come unto me, except it were given unto him of my Father.

John 8.16 And yet if I judge, my judgment is true: for I am not alone, but I and the Father that sent me.

John 8.18 I am one that bear witness of myself, and the Father that sent me beareth witness of me.

John 8.19 Then said they unto him, Where is thy Father? Jesus answered, Ye neither know me, nor my Father: if ye had known me, ye should have known my Father also.

John 8.27 They understood not that he spake to them of the Father.

John 8.28 Then said Jesus unto them, When ye have lifted up the Son of man, then shall ye know that I am [he], and [that] I do nothing of myself; but as my Father hath taught me, I speak these things.

John 8.29 And he that sent me is with me: the Father hath not left me alone; for I do always those things that please him.

John 8.38 I speak that which I have seen with my Father: and ye do that which ye have seen with your father.

John 8.42 Jesus said unto them, If God were your Father, ye would love me: for I proceeded forth and came from God; neither came I of myself, but he sent me.

John 8.49 Jesus answered, I have not a devil; but I honour my Father, and ye do dishonour me.

John 8.54 Jesus answered, If I honour myself, my honour is nothing: it is my Father that honoureth me; of whom ye say, that he is your God:

John 10.15 As the Father knoweth me, even so know I the Father: and I lay down my life for the sheep.

John 10.17 Therefore doth my Father love me, because I lay down my life, that I might take it again.

John 10.18 No man taketh it from me, but I lay it down of myself. I have power to lay it down, and I have power to take it again. This commandment have I received of my Father.

John 10.25 Jesus answered them, I told you, and ye believed not: the works that I do in my Father's name, they bear witness of me.

John 10.29 My Father, which gave [them] me, is greater than all; and no [man] is able to pluck [them] out of my Father's hand.

John 10.30 I and [my] Father are one.

John 10.32 Jesus answered them, Many good works have I showed you from my Father; for which of those works do ye stone me?

John 10.36 Say ye of him, whom the Father hath sanctified, and sent into the world, Thou blasphemest; because I said, I am the Son of God?

John 10.37 If I do not the works of my Father, believe me not.

John 10.38 But if I do, though ye believe not me, believe the works: that ye may know, and believe, that the Father [is] in me, and I in him.

John 11.41 Then they took away the stone [from the place] where the dead was laid. And Jesus lifted up [his] eyes, and said, Father, I thank thee that thou hast heard me.

John 12.26 If any man serve me, let him follow me; and where I am, there shall also my servant be: if any man serve me, him will [my] Father honour.

John 12.27 Now is my soul troubled; and what shall I say? Father, save me from this hour: but for this cause came I unto this hour.

John 12.28 Father, glorify thy name. Then came there a voice from heaven, [saying], I have both glorified [it], and will glorify [it] again.

John 12.49 For I have not spoken of myself; but the Father which sent me, he gave me a commandment, what I should say, and what I should speak.

John 12.50 And I know that his commandment is life everlasting: whatsoever I speak therefore, even as the Father said unto me, so I speak.

John 13.1 Now before the feast of the passover, when Jesus knew that his hour was come that he should depart out of this world unto the Father, having loved his own which were in the world, he loved them unto the end.

John 13.3 Jesus knowing that the Father had given all things into his hands, and that he was come from God, and went to God;

John 14.2 In my Father's house are many mansions: if [it were] not [so], I would have told you. I go to prepare a place for you.

John 14.6 Jesus saith unto him, I am the way, the truth, and the life: no man cometh unto the Father, but by me.

John 14.7 If ye had known me, ye should have known my Father also: and from henceforth ye know him, and have seen him.

John 14.8 Philip saith unto him, Lord, show us the Father, and it sufficeth us.

John 14.9 Jesus saith unto him, Have I been so long time with you, and yet hast thou not known me, Philip? he that hath seen me hath seen the Father; and how sayest thou [then], Show us the Father?

John 14.10 Believest thou not that I am in the Father, and the Father in me? the words that I speak unto you I speak not of myself: but the Father that dwelleth in me, he doeth the works.

John 14.11 Believe me that I [am] in the Father, and the Father in me: or else believe me for the very works' sake.

John 14.12 Verily, verily, I say unto you, He that believeth on me, the works that I do shall he do also; and greater [works] than these shall he do; because I go unto my Father.

John 14.13 And whatsoever ye shall ask in my name, that will I do, that the Father may be glorified in the Son.

John 14.16 And I will pray the Father, and he shall give you another Comforter, that he may abide with you for ever;

John 14.20 At that day ye shall know that I [am] in my Father, and ye in me, and I in you.

John 14.21 He that hath my commandments, and keepeth them, he it is that loveth me: and he that loveth me shall be loved of my Father, and I will love him, and will manifest myself to him.

John 14.23 Jesus answered and said unto him, If a man love me, he will keep my words: and my Father will love him, and we will come unto him, and make our abode with him.

John 14.24 He that loveth me not keepeth not my sayings: and the word which ye hear is not mine, but the Father's which sent me.

John 14.26 But the Comforter, [which is] the Holy Ghost, whom the Father will send in my name, he shall teach you all things, and bring all things to your remembrance, whatsoever I have said unto you.

John 14.28 Ye have heard how I said unto you, I go away, and come [again] unto you. If ye loved me, ye would rejoice, because I said, I go unto the Father: for my Father is greater than I.

John 14.31 But that the world may know that I love the Father; and as the Father gave me commandment, even so I do. Arise, let us go hence.

John 15.1 I am the true vine, and my Father is the husbandman.

John 15.8 Herein is my Father glorified, that ye bear much fruit; so shall ye be my disciples.

John 15.9 As the Father hath loved me, so have I loved you: continue ye in my love.

John 15.10 If ye keep my commandments, ye shall abide in my love; even as I have kept my Father's commandments, and abide in his love.

John 15.15 Henceforth I call you not servants; for the servant knoweth not what his lord doeth: but I have called you friends; for all things that I have heard of my Father I have made known unto you.

John 15.16 Ye have not chosen me, but I have chosen you, and ordained you, that ye should go and bring forth fruit, and [that] your fruit should remain: that whatsoever ye shall ask of the Father in my name, he may give it you.

John 15.23 He that hateth me hateth my Father also.

John 15.24 If I had not done among them the works which none other man did, they had not had sin: but now have they both seen and hated both me and my Father.

John 15.26 But when the Comforter is come, whom I will send unto you from the Father, [even] the Spirit of truth, which proceedeth from the Father, he shall testify of me:

John 16.3 And these things will they do unto you, because they have not known the Father, nor me.

John 16.10 Of righteousness, because I go to my Father, and ye see me no more;

John 16.15 All things that the Father hath are mine: therefore said I, that he shall take of mine, and shall shew [it] unto you.

John 16.16 A little while, and ye shall not see me: and again, a little while, and ye shall see me, because I go to the Father.

John 16.17 Then said [some] of his disciples among themselves, What is this that he saith unto us, A little while, and ye shall not see me: and again, a little while, and ye shall see me: and, Because I go to the Father?

John 16.23 And in that day ye shall ask me nothing. Verily, verily, I say unto you, Whatsoever ye shall ask the Father in my name, he will give [it] you.

John 16.25 These things have I spoken unto you in proverbs: but the time cometh, when I shall no more speak unto you in proverbs, but I shall shew you plainly of the Father.

John 16.26 At that day ye shall ask in my name: and I say not unto you, that I will pray the Father for you:

John 16.27 For the Father himself (tenderly) loveth you, because ye have loved me, and have believed that I came out from God.

John 16.28 I came forth from the Father, and am come into the world: again, I leave the world, and go to the Father.

John 16.32 Behold, the hour cometh, yea, is now come, that ye shall be scattered, every man to his own, and shall leave me alone: and yet I am not alone, because the Father is with me.

John 17.1 These words spake Jesus, and lifted up his eyes to heaven, and said, Father, the hour is come; glorify thy Son, that thy Son also may glorify thee:

John 16.5 And now, O Father, glorify thou me with thine own self with the glory which I had with thee before the world was.

John 16.11 And now I am no more in the world, but these are in the world, and I come to thee. Holy Father, keep through thine own name those whom thou hast given me, that they may be one, as we [are].

John 16.21 That they all may be one; as thou, Father, [art] in me, and I in thee, that they also may be one in us: that the world may believe that thou hast sent me.

John 16.24 Father, I will that they also, whom thou hast given me, be with me where I am; that they may behold my glory, which thou hast given me: for thou lovedst me before the foundation of the world.

John 16.25 O righteous Father, the world hath not known thee: but I have known thee, and these have known that thou hast sent me.

John 18.11 Then said Jesus unto Peter, Put up thy sword into the sheath: the cup which my Father hath given me, shall I not drink it?

John 20.17 Jesus saith unto her, Touch me not; for I am not yet ascended to my Father: but go to my brethren, and say unto them, I ascend unto my Father, and your Father; and [to] my God, and your God.

John 20.21 Then said Jesus to them again, Peace [be] unto you: as [my] Father hath sent me, even so send I you.

Acts 1.4 And, being assembled together with [them], commanded them that they should not depart from Jerusalem, but wait for the promise of the Father, which, [saith he], ye have heard of me.

Acts 1.7 And he said unto them, It is not for you to know the times or the seasons, which the Father hath put in his own power.

Acts 2.33 Therefore being by the right hand of God exalted, and having received of the Father the promise of the Holy Ghost, he hath shed forth this, which ye now see and hear.

Romans 1.7 To all that be in Rome, beloved of God, called [to be] saints: Grace to you and peace from God our Father, and the Lord Jesus Christ.

Romans 6.4 Therefore we are buried with him by baptism into death: that like as Christ was raised up from the dead by the glory of the Father, even so we also should walk in newness of life.

Romans 8.15 For ye have not received the spirit of bondage again to fear; but ye have received the Spirit of adoption, whereby we cry, Abba, Father.

Romans 15.6 That ye may with one mind [and] one mouth glorify God, even the Father of our Lord Jesus Christ.

1 Corinthians 8.6 But to us [there is but] one God, the Father, of whom [are] all things, and we in him; and one Lord Jesus Christ, by whom [are] all things, and we by him.

1 Corinthians 15.24 Then [cometh] the end, when he shall have delivered up the kingdom to God, even the Father; when he shall have put down all rule and all authority and power.

2 Corinthians 1.3 Blessed [be] God, even the Father of our Lord Jesus Christ, the Father of mercies, and the God of all comfort;
2 Corinthians 6.18 And will be a Father unto you, and ye shall be my sons and daughters, saith the Lord Almighty.
Galatians 1.1 Paul, an apostle, (not of men, neither by man, but by Jesus Christ, and God the Father, who raised him from the dead;)
Galatians 1.4 Who gave himself for our sins, that he might deliver us from this present evil world, according to the will of God and our Father:
Galatians 4.6 And because ye are sons, God hath sent forth the Spirit of his Son into your hearts, crying, Abba, Father.
Ephesians 1.3 Blessed [be] the God and Father of our Lord Jesus Christ, who hath blessed us with all spiritual blessings in heavenly [places] in Christ:
Ephesians 1.17 That the God of our Lord Jesus Christ, the Father of glory, may give unto you the spirit of wisdom and revelation in the knowledge of him:
Ephesians 2.18 For through him we both have access by one Spirit unto the Father.
Ephesians 3.14 (prayer) For this cause I bow my knees unto the Father of our Lord Jesus Christ,
Ephesians 4.6 One God and Father of all, who [is] above all, and through all, and in you all.
Ephesians 5.20 Giving thanks always for all things unto God and the Father in the name of our Lord Jesus Christ;
Philippians 2.11 And [that] every tongue should confess that Jesus Christ [is] Lord, to the glory of God the Father.
Colossians 1.12 Giving thanks unto the Father, which hath made us meet to be partakers of the inheritance of the saints in light:
Colossians 1.19 For it pleased [the Father] that in him should all fulness dwell;
1 Thessalonians 1.3 Remembering without ceasing your work of faith, and labour of love, and patience of hope in our Lord Jesus Christ, in the sight of God and our Father;
1 Thessalonians 3.13 To the end he may stablish your hearts unblameable in holiness before God, even our Father, at the coming of our Lord Jesus Christ with all his saints.
2 Thessalonians 2.16 Now our Lord Jesus Christ himself, and God, even our Father, which hath loved us, and hath given [us] everlasting consolation and good hope through grace,
Hebrews 1.5 For unto which of the angels said he at any time, Thou art my Son, this day have I begotten thee? And again, I will be to him a Father, and he shall be to me a Son?
Hebrews 12.9 Furthermore we have had fathers of our flesh which corrected [us], and we gave [them] reverence: shall we not much rather be in subjection unto the Father of spirits, and live?
James 1.17 Every good gift and every perfect gift is from above, and cometh down from the Father of lights, with whom is no variableness, neither shadow of turning.
James 1.27 Pure religion and undefiled before God and the Father is this, To visit the fatherless and widows in their affliction, [and] to keep himself unspotted from the world.
1 Peter 1.2 Elect according to the foreknowledge of God the Father, through sanctification of the Spirit, unto obedience and sprinkling of the blood of Jesus Christ: Grace unto you, and peace, be multiplied.

1 Peter 1.3 Blessed [be] the God and <u>Father</u> of our Lord Jesus Christ, which according to his abundant mercy hath begotten us again unto a lively hope by the resurrection of Jesus Christ from the dead,

1 Peter 1.17 And if ye call on the <u>Father</u>, who without respect of persons judgeth according to every man's work, pass the time of your sojourning [here] in fear:

2 Peter 1.17 For he received from God the <u>Father</u> honour and glory, when there came such a voice to him from the excellent glory, This is my beloved Son, in whom I am well pleased.

1 John 1.2 (For the life was manifested, and we have seen [it], and bear witness, and shew unto you that eternal life, which was with the <u>Father</u>, and was manifested unto us;)

1 John 1.3 That which we have seen and heard declare we unto you, that ye also may have fellowship with us: and truly our fellowship [is] with the <u>Father</u>, and with his Son Jesus Christ.

1 John 2.1 My little children, these things write I unto you, that ye sin not. And if any man sin, we have an advocate with the <u>Father</u>, Jesus Christ the righteous:

1 John 2.13 I write unto you, fathers, because ye have known him [that is] from the beginning. I write unto you, young men, because ye have overcome the wicked one. I write unto you, little children, because ye have known the <u>Father</u>.

1 John 2.15 Love not the world, neither the things [that are] in the world. If any man love the world, the love of the <u>Father</u> is not in him.

1 John 2.16 For all that [is] in the world, the lust of the flesh, and the lust of the eyes, and the pride of life, is not of the <u>Father</u>, but is of the world.

1 John 2.22 Who is a liar but he that denieth that Jesus is the Christ? He is antichrist, that denieth the <u>Father</u> and the Son.

1 John 2.23 Whosoever denieth the Son, the same hath not the <u>Father</u>: [(but) he that acknowledgeth the Son hath the <u>Father</u> also]. **(I acknowledge and receive the Son and <u>Father</u>.)**

1 John 2.24 Let that therefore abide in you, which ye have heard from the beginning. If that which ye have heard from the beginning shall remain in you, ye also shall continue in the Son, and in the <u>Father</u>.

1 John 3.1 Behold, what manner of love the <u>Father</u> hath bestowed upon us, that we should be called the sons of God: therefore the world knoweth us not, because it knew him not.

1 John 4.14 And we have seen and do testify that the <u>Father</u> sent the Son [to be] the Saviour of the world.

1 John 5.7 For there are three that bear record in heaven, the <u>Father</u>, the Word, and the Holy Ghost: and these three are one.

2 John 1.3 Grace be with you, mercy, [and] peace, from God the <u>Father</u>, and from the Lord Jesus Christ, the Son of the <u>Father</u>, in truth and love.

2 John 1.4 I rejoiced greatly that I found of thy children walking in truth, as we have received a commandment from the <u>Father</u>.

2 John 1.9 Whosoever transgresseth, and abideth not in the doctrine of Christ, hath not God. He that abideth in the doctrine of Christ, he hath both the <u>Father</u> and the Son. **(I walk in Truth and abide in the doctrine of Christ, I have Abba and Jesus.)**

Jude 1.1 Jude, the servant of Jesus Christ, and brother of James, to them that are sanctified by God the Father, and preserved in Jesus Christ, [and] called: **(I am sanctified and preserved.)**

Revelation 1.6 And hath made us kings and priests unto God and his Father; to him [be] glory and dominion for ever and ever. Amen.

Revelation 2.27 And he shall rule them with a rod of iron; as the vessels of a potter shall they be broken to shivers: even as I received of my Father.

Revelation 3.5 He that overcometh, the same shall be clothed in white raiment; and I will not blot out his name out of the book of life, but I will confess his name before my Father, and before his angels. **(I'm an overcomer and I receive this blessing.)**

Revelation 3.21 To him that overcometh will I grant to sit with me in my throne, even as I also overcame, and am set down with my Father in his throne. **(I'm an overcomer and will sit with Jesus and Abba on their throne.)**

Revelation 14.1 And I looked, and, lo, a Lamb stood on the mount Sion, and with him an hundred forty [and] four thousand, having his Father's name written in their foreheads. **(I want Father's name on my forehead.)**

CHAPTER 14

DIVINE GUIDANCE

Psalms 23:1 The Lord is my Shepherd: I shall not lack guidance.

John 10 I am his sheep, He is my Shepherd. He leads & guides me.

Matthew 10:20b ...the Spirit of your Father speaketh in you.

Proverbs 6:22 When thou goest, it (the Word) shall lead thee; when thou sleepest, it shall keep thee, and when thou awakest, it shall talk with thee.

Isaiah 50:4-5 The Lord God hath given me the tongue of the learned, that I should know how to speak a word in season to him that is weary: he wakens me morning by morning, he wakens my ear to hear as the learned. The Lord God has opened my ear and I was not rebellious, neither turned away back.

Psalms 16:11 Thou wilt show me the path of life: in thy presence is fullness of joy; at thy right hand there are pleasures for evermore.

Psalms 25:4 Show me thy ways, O Lord; teach me thy paths.
Psalms 25:5 Lead me in thy truth, and teach me: for thou art the God of my salvation: on thee do I wait all the day.
Psalms 25:9 The meek will He guide in judgment: and the meek will He teach His way.
Psalms 25:14 The secret of the Lord is with them that fear Him; and He will show them His covenant.

Psalms 27:11 Teach me thy way, O Lord, and lead me in a plain path, because of my enemies.

Psalms 32:8 I will instruct thee and teach thee in the way which thou shalt go: I will guide (counsel) thee with mine eye (upon you).

Psalms 37:23 The steps of a good man are ordered by the Lord: and he delighteth in his way.

Psalms 48:14 For this God is our God for ever and ever: he will be our guide even unto death.

Psalms 119:34 Give me understanding, and I shall keep thy law; yea, I shall observe it with my whole heart.

Jeremiah 15:16 Thy words were found, and I did eat them; and thy word was unto me the joy and rejoicing of mine heart.

Job 23:12 I have esteemed the words of his mouth more than my necessary food.

Hebrews 11:6 He that comes to God must believe...that He is a rewarder of them that diligently seek Him.

Psalms 119:133 Order my steps in thy word: and let not any iniquity have dominion over me.

Proverbs 3:5 Trust in the Lord with all thine heart; and lean not unto thine own understanding.
Proverbs 3:6 In all thy ways acknowledge him, and he shall direct thy paths.
Proverbs 3:7 Be not wise in thine own eyes: fear the Lord and depart from evil.
Proverbs 3:8 It shall be health to thy navel, and marrow to thy bones.

Proverbs 16:3 Commit thy works unto the Lord, and thy thoughts shall be established.

Proverbs 28:5 Evil men understand not judgment: but they that seek the Lord understand all things.

Isaiah 58:11 And the Lord shall guide thee continually, and satisfy thy soul in drought, and make fat (strong) thy bones: and thou shalt be like a watered garden, and like a spring of water, whose waters fail not.

Jeremiah 10:23 O Lord, I know that the way of man is not in himself: it is not in man that walketh to direct his steps.

John 16:13 Howbeit, when he, the Spirit of truth is come, he will guide you into all truth: for he shall not speak of himself; but whatsoever he shall hear, that shall he speak: and he will show you things to come.

Psalms 73:24 Thou shalt guide me with thy counsel.

Romans 8:14 As many as are led by the Spirit of God, they are the sons of God.

CHAPTER 15

WHAT DO YOU THINK?
YOUR THINKING, THOUGHTS AND IMAGINATIONS

Job 31:1 I made a covenant with mine eyes; why then should I <u>think</u> upon a maid?
Jeremiah 29:11 For I know the <u>thoughts</u> that I <u>think</u> toward you, saith the LORD, <u>thoughts</u> of peace, and not of evil, to give you an expected end.
Matthew 9.4 And Jesus knowing their <u>thoughts</u> said, Wherefore <u>think</u> ye evil in your hearts?
Ephesians 3.20 Now unto him that is able to do exceeding abundantly above all that we ask or <u>think</u>, according to the power that worketh in us,
Philippians 4:8 Finally, brethren, whatsoever things are true, whatsoever things [are] honest, whatsoever things [are] just, whatsoever things [are] pure, whatsoever things [are] lovely, whatsoever things [are] of good report; if [there be] any virtue, and if [there be] any praise, <u>think</u> on these things.

James 1.6 But let him ask in faith, nothing <u>wavering</u>. For he that <u>wavereth</u> is like a wave of the sea driven with the wind and tossed.
James 1.7 For let not that man <u>think</u> that he shall receive any thing of the Lord.
James 1.8 A double minded man is unstable in all his ways.

Proverbs 23:7 For as he <u>thinketh</u> in his heart, so [is] he: Eat and drink, saith he to thee; but his heart [is] not with thee.
1 Corinthians 13:5 (Love) Doth not behave itself unseemly, seeketh not her own, is not easily provoked, <u>thinketh</u> no evil;
Proverbs 24:9 The <u>thought</u> of foolishness [is] sin: and the scorner [is] an abomination to men.
Proverbs 30:32 If thou hast done foolishly in lifting up thyself, or if thou hast <u>thought</u> evil, [lay] thine hand upon thy mouth.
Amos 4:13 For, lo, he that formeth the mountains, and createth the wind, and declareth unto man what [is] his <u>thought</u>, that maketh the morning darkness, and treadeth upon the high places of the earth, The LORD, The God of hosts, [is] his name.
Job 42.2 I know that thou canst do every thing, and that no <u>thought</u> can be withholden from thee.
Psalms 119:59 I <u>thought</u> on my ways, and turned my feet unto thy testimonies.
Psalms 139.2 Thou knowest my downsitting and mine uprising, thou understandest my <u>thought</u> afar off.
Ecclesiastes 10.20 Curse not the king, no not in thy <u>thought</u>; and curse not the rich in thy bedchamber: for a bird of the air shall carry the voice, and that which hath wings shall tell the matter.
Isaiah 14.24 The LORD of hosts hath sworn, saying, Surely as I have <u>thought</u>, so shall it come to pass; and as I have purposed, so shall it stand:

Matthew 6.25 Therefore I say unto you, Take no thought for your life, what ye shall eat, or what ye shall drink; nor yet for your body, what ye shall put on. Is not the life more than meat, and the body than raiment?

2 Corinthians 10:4 (For the weapons of our warfare [are] not carnal, but mighty through God to the pulling down of strongholds;)

2 Corinthians 10:5 Casting down <u>imaginations</u>, and every high thing that exalteth itself against the knowledge of God, and bringing into captivity every <u>thought</u> to the obedience of Christ;

Genesis 6:5 And GOD saw that the wickedness of man [was] great in the earth, and [that] every <u>imagination</u> of the <u>thoughts</u> of his heart [was] only evil continually.

1 Chronicles 28:9 And thou, Solomon my son, know thou the God of thy father, and serve him with a perfect heart and with a willing mind: for the LORD searcheth all hearts, and understandeth all the <u>imaginations</u> of the <u>thoughts</u>: if thou seek him, he will be found of thee; but if thou forsake him, he will cast thee off for ever.

1 Chronicles 29:18 O LORD God of Abraham, Isaac, and of Israel, our fathers, keep this for ever in the <u>imagination</u> of the <u>thoughts</u> of the heart of thy people, and prepare their heart unto thee:

CHAPTER 16

FAITH SCRIPTURES

These scriptures will strengthen your faith and bring you closer to God. When you are feeling depressed, distressed and down in the dumps, read this. God loves you and wants the best for you. Draw near to God and He will draw near to you. Praise Him, love Him, worship Him and sing love songs to Him from your heart. If your life is a mess, ask Him to fix you first, and put you in His perfect will. Stand fast and be faithful to Him.

Regarding the impossibility of Abraham and Sarah to have a child, being very old, God said:
Genesis 18:14 "Is anything too hard for the Lord?"
Unbelief questions God's ability to do what He said He would do.

Hebrews 11:11 By faith Sarah herself also received strength to conceive seed, and she bore a child when she was past the age, because she judged Him faithful who had promised. Therefore from one man, and him as good as dead, were born as many as the stars of the sky…

<u>Romans 4:17-21 New King James Version</u>
(as it is written, "I have made you a father of many nations") in the presence of Him whom he believed – God, who gives life to the dead and calls those things which do not exist as though they did; who, contrary to hope, in hope believed, so that he became the father of many nations, according to what was spoken, "So shall your descendants be."
And not being weak in faith, he did not consider his own body, already dead (since he was about a hundred years old), and the deadness of Sarah's womb.

He did not waver at the promise of God through unbelief, but was strengthened in faith, giving glory to God, and being fully convinced that what He had promised He was also able to perform.

Romans 4:17-21 Amplified Bible
As it is written, I have made you the father of many nations. He was appointed our father – in the sight of God in Whom he believed, Who gives life to the dead and speaks of the non-existent things that [He has foretold and promised] as if they [already] existed. [Genesis 17:5]
[For Abraham, human reason for] hope being gone, hoped on in faith that he should become the father of many nations, as he had been promised, So [numberless] shall your descendants be.
He did not weaken in faith when he considered the [utter] impotence of his own body, which was as good as dead because he was about a hundred years old, or [when he considered] the barrenness of Sarah's (deadened) womb. [Genesis 17:17; 18:11.]
No unbelief or distrust made him waver or doubtingly question concerning the promise of God, but he grew strong and was empowered by faith as he gave praise and glory to God,
Fully satisfied and assured that God was able and mighty to keep His word and to do what He had promised.

Romans 8:11 Amplified version: And if the Spirit of Him Who raised up Jesus from the dead dwells in you, [then] He Who raised up Christ Jesus from the dead will also restore to life your mortal (short-lived, perishable) bodies through His Spirit Who dwells in you.

GOD IS ABLE

2 Corinthians 9:8 And God is able to make all grace abound toward you,…
Ephesians 3:20 God is able to do exceedingly abundantly above all that we ask or think, according to the power that works in us.
Jude 24 God is able to keep you from stumbling
Matthew 9:28 Two blind men came to Jesus. He said, "Do you believe that I am able to do this?"
Daniel 3:17 "Our God whom we serve is able to deliver us from the burning fiery furnace…
Daniel 6:20 "Daniel, has your God… been able to deliver you from the lions?"
Daniel 6:22 My God sent His angel and shut the lions' mouths…
John 11:43 "Lazarus, come forth!" And he who had died came out …
Deuteronomy 11:18 "You shall lay up these words of mine in your heart and in your soul."

NOTHING IS IMPOSSIBLE

Jeremiah 32:17 (Jeremiah said) Ah Lord God! Behold, thou hast made the heaven and the earth by thy great power and stretched out arm, and there is nothing too hard for thee.
Jeremiah 32: 27 (God responded) Behold, I am the Lord, the God of all flesh: is there anything too hard for me?

Matthew 17:20 …and nothing shall be impossible unto you.
Matthew 19:26 …"With men this is impossible, but with God all things are possible."
Mark 10:27 "With men it is impossible, but not with God: for with God all things are possible."
Hebrews 6:18 …it is impossible for God to lie…
Mark 9:23 Jesus said to him, "If you can believe, all things are possible to him who believes."
Mark 14:36 And He said, "Abba, Father, all things are possible for You….
Luke 1:37 For with God nothing will be impossible.
Luke 18:27 But He said, "The things which are impossible with men are possible with God."

SCRIPTURES ON HOPE

Jeremiah 29:11 For I know the thoughts that I think toward you, says the Lord, thoughts of peace and not of evil, to give you a future and a hope.
Jeremiah 29:12 Then you will call upon Me and go and pray to Me, and I will listen to you.
Jeremiah 29:13 And you will seek Me and find Me, when you search for Me with all your heart.

CHAPTER 17

WHAT GOD'S WORD SAYS ABOUT PROSPERITY

INTRODUCTION TO PROSPERITY SCRIPTURES

WARNING!

Do not be deceived by the "Prosperity Gospel" that is being preached. I have been around this message for decades, so I have seen a few things in my time. (I have hesitated for a very long time in making these scriptures public, because I do not want to be labeled as part of the prosperity Gospel, false prophet crowd.)

A friend commented that this prosperity message really took off in the oil-rich areas of Texas and Oklahoma, in cities like Houston, Dallas, and Tulsa, among others. That makes sense, doesn't it? Go where the money is. It's a takeoff on the old Catholic indulgences scam, but instead of paying money for your "get out of Hell free" card to get to go to purgatory instead of hell, they are paying their money for the promise of getting rich and blessed by God. They believe it must be true because the preacher said it.

The preachers of "churchianity" and "religiosity" will use it to promote the satisfying of their own fleshly desires, a bigger home, another car, a bigger boat. It promotes covetousness, their ego, greed and other ungodly things.

They use guilt and condemnation to get you to give beyond your means. This happened recently to a dear Christian friend of mine in Dallas. She had been sick for months and said she knew she was "out of covenant with God" because she could not financially pay her tithe. Even though this is not true, she died and went to her grave believing her rich, Bentley-driving pastor's lies.

Pastor Smiley-Face will say on TV that you can have your best life now by following what he says and give to his ministry. They tell you to think and grow rich, to say out loud every day that "money cometh to me today." Be careful. Preachers are using what I call "Christian Metaphysics" and teachings from the popular metaphysics books to help you learn "the secret" which will bring riches. Jesus said in Matthew chapter 24, "Take heed that you do not be deceived." And I say, "Oops, too late."

Why does the prosperity message work for some and not others? Why do the wicked heathen prosper? One explanation is that Satan is the god of this world. In Luke 4 Satan tempted Jesus with the riches of the world. He told Jesus "all of this has been delivered into my hands and I give it to whoever I want." People have bowed to Satan and have gotten rich, but at the cost of losing their soul.

On the other hand, what are the positive aspects of God's prosperity scriptures?
It will renew your mind to what is possible for your life. As a young man I was verbally beat down and abused. My outlook on life was very bleak. I didn't know what I wanted to be when I grew up. I had a terrible inferiority complex, I was extremely fearful, and I considered myself to be pretty much worthless.

Then after I received God's free love gift for me and became a saved, born again, Holy Spirit-filled Christian, I started reading the Bible and I saw that God says we can have prosperity and blessings if we obey Him and follow His commands. This really intrigued me so I did a Bible study to find all the scriptures that deal with this topic. I meditated on these scriptures and God started to slowly renew my mind and bring me up to a higher level. My thinking changed and my self-esteem rose out of the gutter and more confidence and courage arose in my heart.

Second, it should encourage you to live a godly, righteous life. The scripture says to seek first the kingdom of God and His righteousness – then all these things that you need will then be added to you. Don't put the cart before the horse. Get your priorities straight. Seek God and serve Him with all your heart. He loves you and wants the best for your life.

PROSPERITY SCRIPTURES

The WORD of God is the foundation:
Matthew 6:33 But seek ye first the kingdom of God, and his righteousness; and all these things shall be added unto you.
- This is NOT an overnight "get rich quick" scheme
- Comes by much meditation
- It's free, but it's not cheap

We are made free from the world system and the devil:
John 8:31 Then said Jesus to those Jews which believed on him, If ye continue in my word, then are ye my disciples indeed;

John 8:32 And ye shall know the truth, and the truth shall make you free.
Romans 8:2 For the law of the Spirit of life in Christ Jesus hath made me free from the law of sin and death (and poverty).

I. KNOW THAT IT IS GOD'S WILL FOR US TO PROSPER. GOD'S WORD IS HIS WILL!

3 John 2 Beloved, I wish above all things that thou mayest prosper and be in health, even as thy soul prospereth.
Psalms 35:27 Let them shout for joy, and be glad, that favour my righteous cause: yea, let them say continually, Let the LORD be magnified, which hath pleasure in the prosperity of his servant.

II. BECAUSE OF JESUS' FINISHED WORK AT CALVARY, WE WERE REDEEMED FROM POVERTY UNTO RICHES.

Galatians 3:13 Christ hath redeemed us from the curse of the law, being made a curse for us: for it is written, Cursed is every one that hangeth on a tree:
Galatians 3:14 That the blessing of Abraham might come on the Gentiles through Jesus Christ; that we might receive the promise of the Spirit through faith.
2 Corinthians 8:9 For ye know the grace of our Lord Jesus Christ, that, though he was rich, yet for your sakes he became poor, that ye through his poverty might be rich.
John 10:10 The thief cometh not, but for to steal, and to kill, and to destroy: I am come that they might have life, and that they might have it more abundantly.
Isaiah 53:10 Yet it pleased the LORD to bruise him; he hath put him to grief: when thou shalt make his soul an offering for sin, he shall see his seed, he shall prolong his days, and the pleasure of the LORD shall prosper in his hand.
Isaiah 53:12 Therefore will I divide him a portion with the great, and he shall divide the spoil with the strong; because he hath poured out his soul unto death: and he was numbered with the transgressors; and he bare the sin of many, and made intercession for the transgressors.

III. BECAUSE IT'S OUR INHERITANCE
We Are Now in God's Family; We Have a Rich Father, We Are His Sons

Romans 8:16 The Spirit itself beareth witness with our spirit, that we are the children of God:
Romans 8:17 And if children, then heirs; heirs of God, and joint-heirs with Christ; if so be that we suffer with him, that we may be also glorified together.
Hebews 1:2 Hath in these last days spoken unto us by his Son, whom he hath appointed heir of all things, by whom also he made the worlds;
1 Corinthians 3:21 Therefore let no man glory in men. For all things are yours;
1 Corinthians 3:22 Whether Paul, or Apollos, or Cephas, or the world, or life, or death, or things present, or things to come; all are yours;
1 Corinthians 3:23 And ye are Christ's; and Christ is God's.

Romans 8:32 He that spared not his own Son, but delivered him up for us all, how shall he not with him also freely give us all things? (Since He gave us His most prized possession, surely He will give us lesser things like riches and goods.)

"We are the Bride of Christ; our Father God is the Father of the Bride, and the Father always pays for the expenses."

We are His sheep, Jesus is our Good Shepherd.

Psalms 23:1 The LORD is my shepherd; I shall not want.

Psalms 23:2 He maketh me to lie down in green pastures: he leadeth me beside the still waters.

Psalms 23:3 He restoreth my soul: he leadeth me in the paths of righteousness for his name's sake.

Psalms 23:4 Yea, though I walk through the valley of the shadow of death, I will fear no evil: for thou art with me; thy rod and thy staff they comfort me.

Psalms 23:5 Thou preparest a table before me in the presence of mine enemies: thou anointest my head with oil; my cup runneth over.

Psalms 23:6 Surely goodness and mercy shall follow me all the days of my life: and I will dwell in the house of the LORD for ever.

Matthew 6:19 Lay not up for yourselves treasures upon earth, where moth and rust doth corrupt, and where thieves break through and steal:

Matthew 6:20 But lay up for yourselves treasures in heaven, where neither moth nor rust doth corrupt, and where thieves do not break through nor steal:

Matthew 6:21 For where your treasure is, there will your heart be also.

Matthew 6:22 The light of the body is the eye: if therefore thine eye be single, thy whole body shall be full of light.

Matthew 6:23 But if thine eye be evil, thy whole body shall be full of darkness. If therefore the light that is in thee be darkness, how great is that darkness!

Matthew 6:24 No man can serve two masters: for either he will hate the one, and love the other; or else he will hold to the one, and despise the other. Ye cannot serve God and mammon.

Matthew 6:25 Therefore I say unto you, Take no thought for your life, what ye shall eat, or what ye shall drink; nor yet for your body, what ye shall put on. Is not the life more than meat, and the body than raiment?

Matthew 6:26 Behold the fowls of the air: for they sow not, neither do they reap, nor gather into barns; yet your heavenly Father feedeth them. Are ye not much better than they?

Matthew 6:27 Which of you by taking thought can add one cubit unto his stature?

Matthew 6:28 And why take ye thought for raiment? Consider the lilies of the field, how they grow; they toil not, neither do they spin:

Matthew 6:29 And yet I say unto you, That even Solomon in all his glory was not arrayed like one of these.

Matthew 6:30 Wherefore, if God so clothe the grass of the field, which today is, and tomorrow is cast into the oven, shall he not much more clothe you, O ye of little faith?

Matthew 6:31 Therefore take no thought, saying, What shall we eat? or, What shall we drink? or, Wherewithal shall we be clothed?

Matthew 6:32 (For after all these things do the Gentiles seek:) for your heavenly Father knoweth that ye have need of all these things.

Matthew 6:33 But seek ye first the kingdom of God, and his righteousness; and all these things shall be added unto you.

Matthew 6:34 Take therefore no thought for the morrow: for the morrow shall take thought for the things of itself. Sufficient unto the day is the evil thereof.

Luke 12:13 And one of the company said unto him, Master, speak to my brother, that he divide the inheritance with me.

Luke 12:14 And he said unto him, Man, who made me a judge or a divider over you?

Luke 12:15 And he said unto them, Take heed, and beware of covetousness: for a man's life consisteth not in the abundance of the things which he possesseth.

Luke 12:16 And he spake a parable unto them, saying, The ground of a certain rich man brought forth plentifully:

Luke 12:17 And he thought within himself, saying, What shall I do, because I have no room where to bestow my fruits?

Luke 12:18 And he said, This will I do: I will pull down my barns, and build greater; and there will I bestow all my fruits and my goods.

Luke 12:19 And I will say to my soul, Soul, thou hast much goods laid up for many years; take thine ease, eat, drink, and be merry.

Luke 12:20 But God said unto him, Thou fool, this night thy soul shall be required of thee: then whose shall those things be, which thou hast provided?

Luke 12:21 So is he that layeth up treasure for himself, and is not rich toward God.

Luke 12:22 And he said unto his disciples, Therefore I say unto you, Take no thought for your life, what ye shall eat; neither for the body, what ye shall put on.

Luke 12:23 The life is more than meat, and the body is more than raiment.

Luke 12:24 Consider the ravens: for they neither sow nor reap; which neither have storehouse nor barn; and God feedeth them: how much more are ye better than the fowls?

Luke 12:25 And which of you with taking thought can add to his stature one cubit?

Luke 12:26 If ye then be not able to do that thing which is least, why take ye thought for the rest?

Luke 12:27 Consider the lilies how they grow: they toil not, they spin not; and yet I say unto you, that Solomon in all his glory was not arrayed like one of these.

Luke 12:28 If then God so clothe the grass, which is to day in the field, and tomorrow is cast into the oven; how much more will he clothe you, O ye of little faith?

Luke 12:29 And seek not ye what ye shall eat, or what ye shall drink, neither be ye of doubtful mind.

Luke 12:30 For all these things do the nations of the world seek after: and your Father knoweth that ye have need of these things.

Luke 12:31 But rather seek ye the kingdom of God; and all these things shall be added unto you.

Luke 12:32 Fear not, little flock; for it is your Father's good pleasure to give you the kingdom.

Luke 12:33 Sell that ye have, and give alms; provide yourselves bags which wax not old, a treasure in the heavens that faileth not, where no thief approacheth, neither moth corrupteth.

Luke 12:34 For where your treasure is, there will your heart be also.
Luke 12:35 Let your loins be girded about, and your lights burning;

Deuteronomy 28:1 And it shall come to pass, if thou shalt hearken diligently unto the voice of the LORD thy God, to observe and to do all his commandments which I command thee this day, that the LORD thy God will set thee on high above all nations of the earth:
Deuteronomy 28:2 And all these blessings shall come on thee, and overtake thee, if thou shalt hearken unto the voice of the LORD thy God.
Deuteronomy 28:3 Blessed shalt thou be in the city, and blessed shalt thou be in the field.
Deuteronomy 28:4 Blessed shall be the fruit of thy body, and the fruit of thy ground, and the fruit of thy cattle, the increase of thy kine, and the flocks of thy sheep.
Deuteronomy 28:5 Blessed shall be thy basket and thy store.
Deuteronomy 28:6 Blessed shalt thou be when thou comest in, and blessed shalt thou be when thou goest out.
Deuteronomy 28:7 The LORD shall cause thine enemies that rise up against thee to be smitten before thy face: they shall come out against thee one way, and flee before thee seven ways.
Deuteronomy 28:8 The LORD shall command the blessing upon thee in thy storehouses, and in all that thou settest thine hand unto; and he shall bless thee in the land which the LORD thy God giveth thee.
Deuteronomy 28:9 The LORD shall establish thee an holy people unto himself, as he hath sworn unto thee, if thou shalt keep the commandments of the LORD thy God, and walk in his ways.
Deuteronomy 28:10 And all people of the earth shall see that thou art called by the name of the LORD; and they shall be afraid of thee.
Deuteronomy 28:11 And the LORD shall make thee plenteous in goods, in the fruit of thy body, and in the fruit of thy cattle, and in the fruit of thy ground, in the land which the LORD sware unto thy fathers to give thee.
Deuteronomy 28:12 The LORD shall open unto thee his good treasure, the heaven to give the rain unto thy land in his season, and to bless all the work of thine hand: and thou shalt lend unto many nations, and thou shalt not borrow.
Deuteronomy 28:13 And the LORD shall make thee the head, and not the tail; and thou shalt be above only, and thou shalt not be beneath; if that thou hearken unto the commandments of the LORD thy God, which I command thee this day, to observe and to do them:
Deuteronomy 28:14 And thou shalt not go aside from any of the words which I command thee this day, to the right hand, or to the left, to go after other gods to serve them.

IV. THEY ARE LEGALLY OURS NOW
God Made the Riches for His Children, Not the Devil's Children, And Jesus Legally Gave It Back to Us.

Psalms 24:1 The earth is the LORD'S, and the fulness thereof; the world, and they that dwell therein.
Psalms 50:10 For every beast of the forest is mine, and the cattle upon a thousand hills.
Haggai 2:8 The silver is mine, and the gold is mine, saith the LORD of hosts.

Luke 4:6 And the devil said unto him, All this power will I give thee, and the glory of them: for that is delivered unto me; and to whomsoever I will I give it.

Colossians 2:15 And having spoiled principalities and powers, he made a shew of them openly, triumphing over them in it.

Matthew 28:18 And Jesus came and spake unto them, saying, All power is given unto me in heaven and in earth.

Luke 10:19 Behold, I give unto you power to tread on serpents and scorpions, and over all the power of the enemy: and nothing shall by any means hurt you.

Numbers 33:53 And ye shall dispossess the inhabitants of the land, and dwell therein: for I have given you the land to possess it.

Proverbs 13:22 A good man leaveth an inheritance to his children's children: and the wealth of the sinner is laid up for the just.

Romans 4:13 For the promise, that he should be the heir of the world, was not to Abraham, or to his seed, through the law, but through the righteousness of faith.

Galatians 3:29 And if ye be Christ's, then are ye Abraham's seed, and heirs according to the promise.

Galatians 3:14 That the blessing of Abraham might come on the Gentiles through Jesus Christ; that we might receive the promise of the Spirit through faith.

Ephesians 1:3 Blessed be the God and Father of our Lord Jesus Christ, who hath blessed us with all spiritual blessings in heavenly places in Christ:

Ephesians 1:18 The eyes of your understanding being enlightened; that ye may know what is the hope of his calling, and what the riches of the glory of his inheritance in the saints,

2 Peter 1:3 According as his divine power hath given unto us all things that pertain unto life and godliness, through the knowledge of him that hath called us to glory and virtue:

2 Peter 1:4 Whereby are given unto us exceeding great and precious promises: that by these ye might be partakers of the divine nature, having escaped the corruption that is in the world through lust.

V. SOWING AND REAPING PRINCIPLE

Galatians 6:7 Be not deceived; God is not mocked: for whatsoever a man soweth, that shall he also reap.

Galatians 6:9 And let us not be weary in well doing: for in due season we shall reap, if we faint not.

Luke 6:38 Give, and it shall be given unto you; good measure, pressed down, and shaken together, and running over, shall men give into your bosom. For with the same measure that ye mete withal it shall be measured to you again.

Ecclesiastes 11:1 Cast thy bread upon the waters: for thou shalt find it after many days.

Philippians 4:13 I can do all things through Christ which strengtheneth me.

Philippians 4:14 Notwithstanding ye have well done, that ye did communicate with my affliction.

Philippians 4:15 Now ye Philippians know also, that in the beginning of the gospel, when I departed from Macedonia, no church communicated with me as concerning giving and receiving, but ye only.

Philippians 4:16 For even in Thessalonica ye sent once and again unto my necessity.

Philippians 4:17 Not because I desire a gift: but I desire fruit that may abound to your account.
Philippians 4:18 But I have all, and abound: I am full, having received of Epaphroditus the things which were sent from you, an odour of a sweet smell, a sacrifice acceptable, well pleasing to God.
Philippians 4:19 But my God shall supply all your need according to his riches in glory by Christ Jesus.
2 Corinthians 9:6 But this I say, He which soweth sparingly shall reap also sparingly; and he which soweth bountifully shall reap also bountifully.
2 Corinthians 9:7 Every man according as he purposeth in his heart, so let him give; not grudgingly, or of necessity: for God loveth a cheerful giver.
2 Corinthians 9:8 And God is able to make all grace abound toward you; that ye, always having all sufficiency in all things, may abound to every good work:
2 Corinthians 9:9 (As it is written, He hath dispersed abroad; he hath given to the poor: his righteousness remaineth for ever.
2 Corinthians 9:10 Now he that ministereth seed to the sower both minister bread for your food, and multiply your seed sown, and increase the fruits of your righteousness;)
2 Corinthians 9:11 Being enriched in every thing to all bountifulness, which causeth through us thanksgiving to God.

VI. METHODS OF SOWING

1- Tithing

Malachi 3:10 Bring ye all the tithes into the storehouse, that there may be meat in mine house, and prove me now herewith, saith the LORD of hosts, if I will not open you the windows of heaven, and pour you out a blessing, that there shall not be room enough to receive it.
Malachi 3:11 And I will rebuke the devourer for your sakes, and he shall not destroy the fruits of your ground; neither shall your vine cast her fruit before the time in the field, saith the LORD of hosts.
Proverbs 3:9 Honour the LORD with thy substance, and with the firstfruits of all thine increase:
Proverbs 3:10 So shall thy barns be filled with plenty, and thy presses shall burst out with new wine.

2- Offerings

Luke 6:38 Give, and it shall be given unto you; good measure, pressed down, and shaken together, and running over, shall men give into your bosom. For with the same measure that ye mete withal it shall be measured to you again.

3- Giving to the Gospel

Mark 10:28 Then Peter began to say unto him, Lo, we have left all, and have followed thee.

Mark 10:29 And Jesus answered and said, Verily I say unto you, There is no man that hath left house, or brethren, or sisters, or father, or mother, or wife, or children, or lands, for my sake, and the gospel's,

Mark 10:30 But he shall receive an hundredfold now in this time, houses, and brethren, and sisters, and mothers, and children, and lands, with persecutions; and in the world to come eternal life.

<u>4- Giving to the poor</u>

Proverbs 19:17 He that hath pity upon the poor lendeth unto the LORD; and that which he hath given will he pay him again.

Proverbs 22:9 He that hath a bountiful eye shall be blessed; for he giveth of his bread to the poor.

Proverbs 28:8 He that by usury and unjust gain increaseth his substance, he shall gather it for him that will pity the poor.

Proverbs 28:27 He that giveth unto the poor shall not lack: but he that hideth his eyes shall have many a curse.

VII. COMES BY MEDITATION AND CONFESSION

Joshua 1:8 This book of the law shall not depart out of thy mouth; but thou shalt meditate therein day and night, that thou mayest observe to do according to all that is written therein: for then thou shalt make thy way prosperous, and then thou shalt have good success.

Psalms 1:1 Blessed is the man that walketh not in the counsel of the ungodly, nor standeth in the way of sinners, nor sitteth in the seat of the scornful.

Psalms 1:2 But his delight is in the law of the LORD; and in his law doth he meditate day and night.

Psalms 1:3 And he shall be like a tree planted by the rivers of water, that bringeth forth his fruit in his season; his leaf also shall not wither; and whatsoever he doeth shall prosper.

Romans 10:17 So then faith cometh by hearing, and hearing by the word of God.

VIII. WE GET THEM BY FAITH
Stand on the Word of Blessing. Just Because You Can Believe God's Word Is True, That's Faith. That Faith of Yours Is the Substance of What You Are Hoping for to Come. Hold on to That Faith of Yours, Don't Waver, It Shall Be Manifested.

Hebrews 11:1 Now faith is the substance of things hoped for, the evidence of things not seen.

Mark 11:24 Therefore I say unto you, What things soever ye desire, when ye pray, believe that ye receive them, and ye shall have them.

Hebrews 10:23 Let us hold fast the profession of our faith without wavering; (for he is faithful that promised;)

Hebrews 10:35 Cast not away therefore your confidence, which hath great recompence of reward.

Hebrews 10:36 For ye have need of patience, that, after ye have done the will of God, ye might receive the promise.
James 1:5 If any of you lack wisdom, let him ask of God, that giveth to all men liberally, and upbraideth not; and it shall be given him.
James 1:6 But let him ask in faith, nothing wavering. For he that wavereth is like a wave of the sea driven with the wind and tossed.
James 1:7 For let not that man think that he shall receive any thing of the Lord.
James 1:8 A double minded man is unstable in all his ways.

IX. AS A REWARD FOR HOLDING FAST, FAITHFULNESS

Hebrews 11:6 But without faith it is impossible to please him: for he that cometh to God must believe that he is, and that he is a rewarder of them that diligently seek him.
Psalms 66:12 Thou hast caused men to ride over our heads; we went through fire and through water: but thou broughtest us out into a wealthy place.
Psalms 34:9 O fear the LORD, ye his saints: for there is no want to them that fear him.
Psalms 34:10 The young lions do lack, and suffer hunger: but they that seek the LORD shall not want any good thing.
Psalms 84:11 For the LORD God is a sun and shield: the LORD will give grace and glory: no good thing will he withhold from them that walk uprightly.
Psalms 112:1 Praise ye the LORD. Blessed is the man that feareth the LORD, that delighteth greatly in his commandments.
Psalms 112:2 His seed shall be mighty upon earth: the generation of the upright shall be blessed.
Psalms 112:3 Wealth and riches shall be in his house: and his righteousness endureth for ever.
Proverbs 22:4 By humility and the fear of the LORD are riches, and honour, and life.
Proverbs 15:6 In the house of the righteous is much treasure: but in the revenues of the wicked is trouble.
Proverbs 8:20 I lead in the way of righteousness, in the midst of the paths of judgment:
Proverbs 8:21 That I may cause those that love me to inherit substance; and I will fill their treasures.
Proverbs 28:10 Whoso causeth the righteous to go astray in an evil way, he shall fall himself into his own pit: but the upright shall have good things in possession.
Proverbs 28:20 A faithful man shall abound with blessings: but he that maketh haste to be rich shall not be innocent.
Proverbs 28:25 He that is of a proud heart stirreth up strife: but he that putteth his trust in the LORD shall be made fat.

X. I KNOW HE IS ABLE, BUT WILL HE DO IT FOR ME?
**Is He Willing? Yes, Because He Already Has Done It, Legally,
in the Spiritual Realm, but You Must Stand on the Word of Blessing to Have It Experientially, in the Physical Realm.**

Psalms 68:19 Blessed be the Lord, who daily loadeth us with benefits, even the God of our salvation. Selah.

1 Timothy 6:17 Charge them that are rich in this world, that they be not highminded, nor trust in uncertain riches, but in the living God, who giveth us richly all things to enjoy;

Luke 12:32 Fear not, little flock; for it is your Father's good pleasure to give you the kingdom.

Proverbs 10:22 The blessing of the LORD, it maketh rich, and he addeth no sorrow with it.

Psalms 37:4 Delight thyself also in the LORD; and he shall give thee the desires of thine heart.

Deuteronomy 8:18 But thou shalt remember the LORD thy God: for it is he that giveth thee power to get wealth, that he may establish his covenant which he sware unto thy fathers, as it is this day.

3 John 1:2 Beloved, I wish above all things that thou mayest prosper and be in health, even as thy soul prospereth.

CHAPTER 18

WHAT GOD'S WORD SAYS ABOUT THE OCCULT, PSYCHICS & WITCHCRAFT

**The following terms and practices are of the devil.
They are satanic and must be renounced and avoided:**

Sorcery, astrology, witchcraft, black arts, materializations, tea leaves, levitation, palmistry, palm reading, Scientology, white magic, colorology, black mass, phrenology, I Ching, ESP, kabala, divination, Ouija boards, fortune-telling, satan worship, spiritualism, parapsychology, numerology, table tipping, tarot cards, clairvoyance, psychics, the Illuminati, alchemy, voodoo, talismans, telepathy, fetishes, seances, automatic writing, clairaudience, UFOs, pendulum healing, channeling, psychic portraits, crystal gazing, dream analysis, Rosicrucianism, Freemasonry (Masonic Lodges), yoga meditation, reincarnation, devil's pentagram, person programming, satanic ritual abuse, Monarch mind control programming (MK-Ultra), astral projection, transcendental meditation, psychic healing, and many more …

DEFINITIONS OF OCCULT WORDS USED IN THE BIBLE

<u>Divination</u>: fortuneteller, crystal ball reader, palm reader, tarot card reader
<u>An observer of times</u>: soothsayer, which is the act of foretelling events, prediction, also astrology, horoscopes, zodiac
<u>enchanter</u>: magician, hypnotist
<u>witch</u>: sorceress, medium, seances, voodoo, a *traiteur* (treater/healer) in south Louisiana
<u>charmer</u>: hypnotist, medals, good luck charms, superstition
<u>consulter with familiar spirits</u>: a medium possessed with a spirit or "guide"; ouija board, automatic writing; tarot cards
<u>wizard</u>: clairvoyant or psychic; magician
<u>necromancer</u>: medium who consults the dead
<u>pass through the fire</u>: to be burned alive as an offering to Molech, one of their gods
<u>sorcery</u>: from the Greek word pharmakia, from which we get the word pharmacy; dealing with the use of drugs to perform witchcraft, to command demons, cast spells, etc.

augur: an official diviner of ancient Rome; soothsayer; to foretell from omens
augury: divination from omens or portents or from chance events, as in the fall of lots
portent: something that foreshadows a coming event

Deuteronomy 18:9 When thou art come into the land which the LORD thy God giveth thee, thou shalt not learn to do after the abominations of those nations.
Deuteronomy 18:10 There shall not be found among you any one that maketh his son or his daughter to pass through the fire, or that useth divination (fortuneteller, crystal ball reader, palm reader, tarot card reader), or an observer of times (soothsayer, which is the act of foretelling events, prediction, also astrology, horoscopes, zodiac) or an enchanter (magician, hypnotist) or a witch (sorceress, medium, seances, voodoo, traiteur),
Deuteronomy 18:11 Or a charmer (hypnotist, medals, good luck charms, superstition), or a consulter with familiar spirits (a medium possessed with a spirit or "guide"; ouija board, automatic writing), or a wizard (clairvoyant or psychic; magician), or a necromancer (medium who consults the dead).
Deuteronomy 18:12 For all that do these things are an abomination unto the LORD: and because of these abominations the LORD thy God doth drive them out from before thee.
Deuteronomy 18:13 Thou shalt be perfect with the LORD thy God
Deuteronomy 18:14 For these nations, which thou shalt possess, hearkened unto observers of times, and unto diviners: but as for thee, the LORD thy God hath not suffered (permitted) thee so to do.

Exodus 7:10b and Aaron cast down his rod before Pharaoh, and before his servants, and it became a serpent.
Exodus 7:11 Then Pharaoh also called the wise men and the sorcerers: now the magicians of Egypt, they also did in like manner with their enchantments.
Exodus 7:12 For they cast down every man his rod, and they became serpents: but Aaron's rod swallowed up their rods.

Exodus 8:18 And the magicians did so with their enchantments to bring forth lice, but they could not: so there were lice upon man, and upon beast.
Exodus 8:19 Then the magicians said unto Pharaoh, This is the finger of God: and Pharaoh's heart was hardened, and he hearkened not unto them; as the LORD had said.

2 Timothy 3:8 Now as Jannes and Jambres withstood Moses, so do these also resist the truth: men of corrupt minds, reprobate concerning the faith.

Exodus 22:18 Thou shalt not permit a witch to live.

Leviticus 19:26 neither shall ye use enchantment, nor observe times.
Leviticus 19:31 Regard not them that have familiar spirits, neither seek after wizards, to be defiled by them: I am the LORD your God.

Leviticus 19:26 (Amplified Bible) … neither shall you use magic, omens or witchcraft, or predict events by horoscope or signs and lucky days.

Leviticus 19:31 Turn not to those mediums who have familiar spirits, or to wizards; do not seek them out to be defiled by them. I am the LORD your God.

Leviticus 20:6 And the soul that turneth after such as have familiar spirits, and after wizards, to go a whoring after them, I will even set my face against that soul, and will cut him off from among his people.

Leviticus 20:6 (Amplified) The person who turns to those who have familiar spirits and to wizards, [being unfaithful to Israel's Maker Who is her Husband, and thus] playing the harlot after them, I will set my face against that person and will cut him off from among his people [that he may not be included in the atonement made for them].

Leviticus 20:27 A man also or woman that hath a familiar spirit (who is a medium), or that is a wizard, shall surely be put to death: they shall stone them with stones: their blood shall be upon them.

1 Samuel 28:3-20 The story of King Saul's visit to the witch at Endor:

3 Now Samuel was dead, and all Israel had lamented him, and buried him in Ramah, even in his own city. And Saul had put away those that had familiar spirits, and the wizards, out of the land.

4 And the Philistines gathered themselves together and came and pitched in Shunem: and Saul gathered all Israel together, and they pitched in Gilboa.

5 And when Saul saw the host of the Philistines, he was afraid, and his heart greatly trembled.

6 And when Saul enquired of the LORD, the LORD answered him not, neither by dreams, nor by Urim, nor by prophets.

7 Then said Saul unto his servants, Seek me a woman that hath a familiar spirit, that I may go to her, and enquire of her. And his servants said to him, Behold, there is a woman that hath a familiar spirit at Endor.

8 And Saul disguised himself, and put on other raiment, and he went, and two men with him, and they came to the woman by night: and he said, I pray thee, divine unto me by the familiar spirit, and bring me him up, whom I shall name unto thee.

9 And the woman said unto him, Behold, thou knowest what Saul hath done, how he hath cut off those that have familiar spirits, and the wizards, out of the land: wherefore then layest thou a snare for my life, to cause me to die?

10 And Saul sware to her by the LORD, saying, As the LORD liveth, there shall no punishment happen to thee for this thing.

11 Then said the woman, Whom shall I bring up unto thee? And he said, Bring me up Samuel.

12 And when the woman saw Samuel, she cried with a loud voice: and the woman spake to Saul, saying, Why hast thou deceived me? for thou art Saul.

13 And the king said unto her, Be not afraid: for what sawest thou? And the woman said unto Saul, I saw gods ascending out of the earth.

14 And he said unto her, What form is he of? And she said, An old man cometh up; and he is covered with a mantle. And Saul perceived that it was Samuel, and he stooped with his face to the ground, and bowed himself.

15 And Samuel said to Saul, Why hast thou disquieted me, to bring me up? And Saul answered, I am sore distressed; for the Philistines make war against me, and God is departed from me, and answereth me no more, neither by prophets, nor by dreams: therefore I have called thee, that thou mayest make known unto me what I shall do.

16 Then said Samuel, Wherefore then dost thou ask of me, seeing the LORD is departed from thee, and is become thine enemy?

17 And the LORD hath done to him, as he spake by me: for the LORD hath rent the kingdom out of thine hand, and given it to thy neighbour, even to David:

18 Because thou obeyedst not the voice of the LORD, nor executedst his fierce wrath upon Amalek, therefore hath the LORD done this thing unto thee this day.

19 Moreover the LORD will also deliver Israel with thee into the hand of the Philistines: and tomorrow shalt thou and thy sons be with me: the LORD also shall deliver the host of Israel into the hand of the Philistines.

20 Then Saul fell straightway all along on the earth, and was sore afraid, because of the words of Samuel: and there was no strength in him; for he had eaten no bread all the day, nor all the night.

1 Chronicles 10:13 So Saul died for his transgression which he committed against the LORD, even against the word of the LORD, which he kept not, and also for asking counsel of one that had a familiar spirit, to enquire of it;

1 Chronicles 10:14 And enquired not of the LORD: therefore he slew him, and turned the kingdom unto David the son of Jesse.

2 Kings 21: 6 King Manasseh made his son pass through the fire [and burned him as an offering to Molech], and observed times [he practiced soothsaying and augury], and used enchantments, and dealt with familiar spirits [mediums] and wizards: he wrought much wickedness in the sight of the LORD, to provoke Him to anger.

Isaiah 2:6 You have rejected your people, because they are filled with customs from the East and with soothsayers who foretell like the Philistines.

Isaiah 8:19 And when the people [instead of putting their trust in God] shall say to you, "Consult for direction mediums [those that have familiar spirits] and wizards who peep and mutter," should not a people seek and consult their God? Should they consult the dead on behalf of the living?

Jeremiah 27:9 Therefore hearken not ye to your prophets, nor to your diviners, nor to your dreamers, nor to your enchanters, nor to your sorcerers, which speak unto you, saying, Ye shall not serve the king of Babylon:

Jeremiah 27:10 For they prophesy a lie unto you, to remove you far from your land; and that I should drive you out, and ye should perish.

Zechariah 10:2 For the teraphim [household idols] have spoken vanity – emptiness, falsity and futility – and the diviners have seen a lie and the dreamers have told false dreams; they comfort in vain. Therefore the people go their way like sheep, they are afflicted and hurt because there is no shepherd.

Revelation 21:8 But the fearful, and unbelieving, and the abominable, and murderers, and whoremongers, and sorcerers, and idolaters, and all liars, shall have their part in the lake which burns with fire and brimstone: which is the second death.

Isaiah 47: 9 But these two things shall come to thee in a moment in one day, the loss of children, and widowhood: they shall come upon thee in their perfection for the multitude of thy sorceries, and for the great abundance of thine enchantments.

Isaiah 47:10 For thou hast trusted in thy wickedness: thou hast said, "None seeth me." Thy wisdom and thy knowledge, it hath perverted thee; and thou hast said in thine heart, "I am, and none else beside me."

Isaiah 47:13 Thou art wearied in the multitude of thy counsels. Let now the astrologers, the stargazers, the monthly prognosticators, stand up, and save thee from these things that shall come upon thee.

CHAPTER 19

JESUS ROSE FROM THE DEAD

Here are Bible scriptures proving that Almighty God raised our Lord Jesus Christ from the dead. The verses were obtained by doing a word search of the Strong's Concordance using the free online tool called BlueLetterBible.org.

Raised

Acts 2:24 Whom God hath raised up, having loosed the pains of death: because it was not possible that he should be holden of it.

Acts 2:32 This Jesus hath God raised up, whereof we all are witnesses.

Acts 3:15 And killed the Prince of life, whom God hath raised from the dead; whereof we are witnesses.

Acts 3:26 Unto you first God, having raised up his Son Jesus, sent him to bless you, in turning away every one of you from his iniquities.

Acts 4:10 Be it known unto you all, and to all the people of Israel, that by the name of Jesus Christ of Nazareth, whom ye crucified, whom God raised from the dead, [even] by him doth this man stand here before you whole.

Acts 5:30 The God of our fathers raised up Jesus, whom ye slew and hanged on a tree.

Acts 10:40 Him God raised up the third day, and shewed him openly;

Acts 13:30 But God raised him from the dead:

Acts 13:33 God hath fulfilled the same unto us their children, in that he hath raised up Jesus again; as it is also written in the second psalm, Thou art my Son, this day have I begotten thee.

Acts 13:34 And as concerning that he raised him up from the dead, [now] no more to return to corruption, he said on this wise, I will give you the sure mercies of David.

Acts 13:37 But he, whom God raised again, saw no corruption.

Acts 17:31 Because he hath appointed a day, in the which he will judge the world in righteousness by [that] man whom he hath ordained; [whereof] he hath given assurance unto all [men], in that he hath raised him from the dead.

Romans 4:24 But for us also, to whom it shall be imputed, if we believe on him that <u>raised</u> up Jesus our Lord from the dead;

Romans 4:25 Who was delivered for our offences, and was <u>raised</u> again for our justification.

Romans 6:4 Therefore we are buried with him by baptism into death: that like as Christ was <u>raised</u> up from the dead by the glory of the Father, even so we also should walk in newness of life.

Romans 6:9 Knowing that Christ being <u>raised</u> from the dead dieth no more; death hath no more dominion over him.

Romans 7:4 Wherefore, my brethren, ye also are become dead to the law by the body of Christ; that ye should be married to another, [even] to him who is <u>raised</u> from the dead, that we should bring forth fruit unto God.

Romans 8:11 But if the Spirit of him that <u>raised</u> up Jesus from the dead dwell in you, he that <u>raised</u> up Christ from the dead shall also quicken your mortal bodies by his Spirit that dwelleth in you.

Romans 10:9 That if thou shalt confess with thy mouth the Lord Jesus, and shalt believe in thine heart that God hath <u>raised</u> him from the dead, thou shalt be saved.

1 Corinthians 6:14 And God hath both <u>raised</u> up the Lord, and will also <u>raise</u> up us by his own power.

1 Corinthians 15:15 Yea, and we are found false witnesses of God; because we have testified of God that he <u>raised</u> up Christ: whom he <u>raised</u> not up, if so be that the dead rise not.

1 Corinthians 15:16 For if the dead rise not, then is not Christ <u>raised</u>:

1 Corinthians 15:17 And if Christ be not <u>raised</u>, your faith [is] vain; ye are yet in your sins.

2 Corinthians 4:14 Knowing that he which <u>raised</u> up the Lord Jesus shall <u>raise</u> up us also by Jesus, and shall present [us] with you.

Galatians 1:1 Paul, an apostle, (not of men, neither by man, but by Jesus Christ, and God the Father, who <u>raised</u> him from the dead;)

Ephesians 1:20 Which he wrought in Christ, when he <u>raised</u> him from the dead, and set [him] at his own right hand in the heavenly [places],

Ephesians 2:4 But God, who is rich in mercy, for his great love wherewith he loved us,

Ephesians 2:5 Even when we were dead in sins, hath quickened us together with Christ, (by grace ye are saved;)

Ephesians 2:6 And hath <u>raised</u> [us] up together, and made [us] sit together in heavenly [places] in Christ Jesus:

Colossians 2:12 Buried with him in baptism, wherein also ye are <u>risen</u> with [him] through the faith of the operation of God, who hath <u>raised</u> him from the dead.

1 Thessalonians 1:10 And to wait for his Son from heaven, whom he <u>raised</u> from the dead, [even] Jesus, which delivered us from the wrath to come.

2 Timothy 2:8 Remember that Jesus Christ of the seed of David was <u>raised</u> from the dead according to my gospel:

1 Peter 1:21 Who by him do believe in God, that <u>raised</u> him up from the dead, and gave him glory; that your faith and hope might be in God.

Resurrection

Matthew 27:52 And the graves were opened; and many bodies of the saints which slept arose,

Matthew 27:53 And came out of the graves after his resurrection, and went into the holy city, and appeared unto many.

John 11:25 Jesus said unto her, I am the resurrection, and the life: he that believeth in me, though he were dead, yet shall he live:

Acts 1:22 Beginning from the baptism of John, unto that same day that he was taken up from us, must one be ordained to be a witness with us of his resurrection.

Acts 2:31 He seeing this before spake of the resurrection of Christ, that his soul was not left in hell, neither his flesh did see corruption.

Acts 2:32 This Jesus hath God raised up, whereof we all are witnesses.

Acts 2:33 Therefore being by the right hand of God exalted, and having received of the Father the promise of the Holy Ghost, he hath shed forth this, which ye now see and hear.

Acts 2:34 For David is not ascended into the heavens: but he saith himself, The LORD said unto my Lord, Sit thou on my right hand,

Acts 2:35 Until I make thy foes thy footstool.

Acts 2:36 Therefore let all the house of Israel know assuredly, that God hath made that same Jesus, whom ye have crucified, both Lord and Christ.

Acts 4:2 Being grieved that they taught the people, and preached through Jesus the resurrection from the dead.

Acts 4:33 And with great power gave the apostles witness of the resurrection of the Lord Jesus: and great grace was upon them all.

Acts 17:18 Then certain philosophers of the Epicureans, and of the Stoicks, encountered him. And some said, What will this babbler say? other some, He seemeth to be a setter forth of strange gods: because he preached unto them Jesus, and the resurrection.

Romans 1:4 And declared [to be] the Son of God with power, according to the spirit of holiness, by the resurrection from the dead:

Romans 6:5 For if we have been planted together in the likeness of his death, we shall be also [in the likeness] of [his] resurrection:

1 Corinthians 15:12 Now if Christ be preached that he rose from the dead, how say some among you that there is no resurrection of the dead?

1 Corinthians 15:13 But if there be no resurrection of the dead, then is Christ not risen:

1 Corinthians 15:14 And if Christ be not risen, then [is] our preaching vain, and your faith [is] also vain.

1 Corinthians 15:15 Yea, and we are found false witnesses of God; because we have testified of God that he raised up Christ: whom he raised not up, if so be that the dead rise not.

1 Corinthians 15:16 For if the dead rise not, then is not Christ raised:

1 Corinthians 15:17 And if Christ be not raised, your faith [is] vain; ye are yet in your sins.

1 Corinthians 15:18 Then they also which are fallen asleep in Christ are perished.

1 Corinthians 15:19 If in this life only we have hope in Christ, we are of all men most miserable.

1 Corinthians 15:20 But now is Christ risen from the dead, [and] become the firstfruits of them that slept.

1 Corinthians 15:21 For since by man [came] death, by man [came] also the <u>resurrection</u> of the dead.

1 Corinthians 15:22 For as in Adam all die, even so in Christ shall all be made alive.

1 Corinthians 15:23 But every man in his own order: Christ the firstfruits; afterward they that are Christ's at his coming.

1 Corinthians 15:24 Then [cometh] the end, when he shall have delivered up the kingdom to God, even the Father; when he shall have put down all rule and all authority and power.

Philippians 3:10 That I may know him, and the power of his <u>resurrection</u>, and the fellowship of his sufferings, being made conformable unto his death;

Philippians 3:11 If by any means I might attain unto the <u>resurrection</u> of the dead.

1 Peter 1:3 Blessed [be] the God and Father of our Lord Jesus Christ, which according to his abundant mercy hath begotten us again unto a lively hope by the <u>resurrection</u> of Jesus Christ from the dead,

1 Peter 3:21 The like figure whereunto [even] baptism doth also now save us (not the putting away of the filth of the flesh, but the answer of a good conscience toward God,) by the <u>resurrection</u> of Jesus Christ:

1 Peter 3:22 Who is gone into heaven, and is on the right hand of God; angels and authorities and powers being made subject unto him.

<u>Raise</u>

Acts 26:8 Why should it be thought a thing incredible with you, that God should <u>raise</u> the dead?

1 Corinthians 6:14 And God hath both <u>raised</u> up the Lord, and will also <u>raise</u> up us by his own power.

2 Corinthians 4:14 Knowing that he which <u>raised</u> up the Lord Jesus shall <u>raise</u> up us also by Jesus, and shall present [us] with you.

<u>Raiseth</u>

John 5:21 For as the Father <u>raiseth</u> up the dead, and quickeneth [them]; even so the Son quickeneth whom he will.

2 Corinthians 1:9 But we had the sentence of death in ourselves, that we should not trust in ourselves, but in God which <u>raiseth</u> the dead:

<u>Rise</u>

Matthew 20:19 And shall deliver him to the Gentiles to mock, and to scourge, and to crucify [him]: and the third day he shall <u>rise</u> again.

Matthew 27:63 Saying, Sir, we remember that that deceiver said, while he was yet alive, After three days I will <u>rise</u> again.

Mark 8:31 And he began to teach them, that the Son of man must suffer many things, and be rejected of the elders, and [of] the chief priests, and scribes, and be killed, and after three days <u>rise</u> again.

Mark 9:31 For he taught his disciples, and said unto them, The Son of man is delivered into the hands of men, and they shall kill him; and after that he is killed, he shall <u>rise</u> the third day.

Mark 10:34 And they shall mock him, and shall scourge him, and shall spit upon him, and shall kill him: and the third day he shall <u>rise</u> again.

Luke 18:33 And they shall scourge [him], and put him to death: and the third day he shall <u>rise</u> again.

Luke 24:7 Saying, The Son of man must be delivered into the hands of sinful men, and be crucified, and the third day <u>rise</u> again.

Luke 24:46 And said unto them, Thus it is written, and thus it behoved Christ to suffer, and to <u>rise</u> from the dead the third day:

John 20:9 For as yet they knew not the scripture, that he must <u>rise</u> again from the dead.

Acts 26:23 That Christ should suffer, [and] that he should be the first that should <u>rise</u> from the dead, and should shew light unto the people, and to the Gentiles.

<u>Risen</u>

Matthew 17:9 And as they came down from the mountain, Jesus charged them, saying, Tell the vision to no man, until the Son of man be <u>risen</u> again from the dead.

Matthew 26:32 But after I am <u>risen</u> again, I will go before you into Galilee.

Matthew 27:64 Command therefore that the sepulchre be made sure until the third day, lest his disciples come by night, and steal him away, and say unto the people, He is <u>risen</u> from the dead: so the last error shall be worse than the first.

Matthew 28:5 And the angel answered and said unto the women, Fear not ye: for I know that ye seek Jesus, which was crucified.

Matthew 28:6 He is not here: for he is <u>risen</u>, as he said. Come, see the place where the Lord lay.

Matthew 28:7 And go quickly, and tell his disciples that he is <u>risen</u> from the dead; and, behold, he goeth before you into Galilee; there shall ye see him: lo, I have told you.

Mark 9:9 And as they came down from the mountain, he charged them that they should tell no man what things they had seen, till the Son of man were <u>risen</u> from the dead.

Mark 9:10 And they kept that saying with themselves, questioning one with another what the <u>rising</u> from the dead should mean.

Mark 14:28 But after that I am <u>risen</u>, I will go before you into Galilee.

Mark 16:3 And they said among themselves, Who shall roll us away the stone from the door of the sepulchre?

Mark 16:4 And when they looked, they saw that the stone was rolled away: for it was very great.

Mark 16:5 And entering into the sepulchre, they saw a young man sitting on the right side, clothed in a long white garment; and they were affrighted.

Mark 16:6 And he saith unto them, Be not affrighted: Ye seek Jesus of Nazareth, which was crucified: he is <u>risen</u>; he is not here: behold the place where they laid him.

Mark 16:7 But go your way, tell his disciples and Peter that he goeth before you into Galilee: there shall ye see him, as he said unto you.

Mark 16:8 And they went out quickly, and fled from the sepulchre; for they trembled and were amazed: neither said they any thing to any [man]; for they were afraid.

Mark 16:9 Now when [Jesus] was <u>risen</u> early the first [day] of the week, he appeared first to Mary Magdalene, out of whom he had cast seven devils.

Mark 16:14 Afterward he appeared unto the eleven as they sat at meat, and upbraided them with their unbelief and hardness of heart, because they believed not them which had seen him after he was <u>risen</u>.

Luke 24:6 He is not here, but is <u>risen</u>: remember how he spake unto you when he was yet in Galilee,

Luke 24:33 And they rose up the same hour, and returned to Jerusalem, and found the eleven gathered together, and them that were with them,

Luke 24:34 Saying, The Lord is <u>risen</u> indeed, and hath appeared to Simon.

John 2:20 Then said the Jews, Forty and six years was this temple in building, and wilt thou rear it up in three days?

John 2:21 But he spake of the temple of his body.

John 2:22 When therefore he was <u>risen</u> from the dead, his disciples remembered that he had said this unto them; and they believed the scripture, and the word which Jesus had said.

John 21:14 This is now the third time that Jesus shewed himself to his disciples, after that he was <u>risen</u> from the dead.

Acts 17:3 Opening and alleging, that Christ must needs have suffered, and <u>risen</u> again from the dead; and that this Jesus, whom I preach unto you, is Christ.

Romans 8:34 Who [is] he that condemneth? [It is] Christ that died, yea rather, that is <u>risen</u> again, who is even at the right hand of God, who also maketh intercession for us.

Colossians 3:1 If ye then be <u>risen</u> with Christ, seek those things which are above, where Christ sitteth on the right hand of God.

<u>Rising</u>

Mark 9:10 And they kept that saying with themselves, questioning one with another what the <u>rising</u> from the dead should mean.

<u>Miscellaneous</u>

Hebrews 13:20 Now the God of peace, that <u>brought again from the dead</u> our Lord Jesus, that great shepherd of the sheep, through the blood of the everlasting covenant,

Revelation 1:5 And from Jesus Christ, [who is] the faithful witness, [and] the <u>first begotten of the dead</u>, and the prince of the kings of the earth. Unto him that loved us, and washed us from our sins in his own blood,

Revelation 1:8 I am Alpha and Omega, the beginning and the ending, saith the Lord, which is, and which was, and which is to come, the Almighty.

Revelation 1:18 I [am] <u>he that liveth</u>, and <u>was dead</u>; and, behold, <u>I am alive</u> for evermore, Amen; and have the keys of hell and of death.

Revelation 2:8 And unto the angel of the church in Smyrna write; These things saith the first and the last, which <u>was dead</u>, <u>and is alive</u>;

Revelation 3:21 To him that overcometh will I grant to sit with me in my throne, even as I also overcame, and am set down with my Father in his throne.
Acts 25:19 But had certain questions against him of their own superstition, and of one Jesus, which was dead, whom Paul affirmed to be alive.
Mark 16:11 And they, when they had heard that he was alive, and had been seen of her, believed not.

Luke 24:23 And when they found not his body, they came, saying, that they had also seen a vision of angels, which said that he was alive.
Luke 24:24 And certain of them which were with us went to the sepulchre, and found [it] even so as the women had said: but him they saw not.
Luke 24:25 Then he said unto them, O fools, and slow of heart to believe all that the prophets have spoken:
Luke 24:26 Ought not Christ to have suffered these things, and to enter into his glory?

Acts 1:3 To whom also he showed himself alive after his passion by many infallible proofs, being seen of them forty days, and speaking of the things pertaining to the kingdom of God:
1 Peter 3:18 For Christ also hath once suffered for sins, the just for the unjust, that he might bring us to God, being put to death in the flesh, but quickened by the Spirit:
1 Peter 3:19 By which also he went and preached unto the spirits in prison;
Matthew 27:50 Jesus, when he had cried again with a loud voice, yielded up the ghost.
Matthew 27:51 And, behold, the veil of the temple was rent in twain from the top to the bottom; and the earth did quake, and the rocks rent;
Matthew 27:52 And the graves were opened; and many bodies of the saints which slept arose,(These are the Firstfruits.)
Matthew 27:53 And came out of the graves after his resurrection, and went into the holy city, and appeared unto many.

CHAPTER 20

THE LIGHT OF THE BODY IS THE EYE

Here are some scriptures that need to be studied and meditated on so we can beware of what we allow to enter our eye gates. Do not allow darkness to enter in, otherwise it will affect your entire being. There are two Bible passages with various versions listed to give a clearer explanation of each.

KING JAMES VERSION
Matthew 6.22 The light of the body is the eye: if therefore thine eye be single, thy whole body shall be full of light. 23 But if thine eye be evil, thy whole body shall be full of darkness. If therefore the light that is in thee be darkness, how great is that darkness!

AMPLIFIED BIBLE (AMP)
Matthew 6.22 "The eye is the lamp of the body; so if your eye is clear [spiritually perceptive], your whole body will be full of light [benefiting from God's precepts]. 23 But if your eye is bad [spiritually blind], your whole body will be full of darkness

[devoid of God's precepts]. So if the [very] light inside you [your inner self, your heart, your conscience] is darkness, how great and terrible is that darkness!

LIVING BIBLE
Matthew 6.22 "If your eye is pure, there will be sunshine in your soul. 23 But if your eye is clouded with evil thoughts and desires, you are in deep spiritual darkness. And oh, how deep that darkness can be!

THE MESSAGE
Matthew 6.22-23 "Your eyes are windows into your body. If you open your eyes wide in wonder and belief, your body fills up with light. If you live squinty-eyed in greed and distrust, your body is a dank cellar. If you pull the blinds on your windows, what a dark life you will have!

NEW INTERNATIONAL READERS VERSION (NIRV)
Matthew 6.22 "The eye is like a lamp for the body. Suppose your eyes are healthy. Then your whole body will be full of light. 23 But suppose your eyes can't see well. Then your whole body will be full of darkness. If the light inside you is darkness, then it is very dark!

NEW LIVING TRANSLATION (NLT)
Matthew 6.22 "Your eye is a lamp that provides light for your body. When your eye is good, your whole body is filled with light. 23 But when your eye is bad, your whole body is filled with darkness. And if the light you think you have is actually darkness, how deep that darkness is!

THE VOICE (VOICE)
Matthew 6.22 The eye is the lamp of the body. You draw light into your body through your eyes, and light shines out to the world through your eyes. So if your eye is well and shows you what is true, then your whole body will be filled with light. 23 But if your eye is clouded or evil, then your body will be filled with evil and dark clouds. And the darkness that takes over the body of a child of God who has gone astray—that is the deepest, darkest darkness there is.

WORLDWIDE ENGLISH (NEW TESTAMENT) (WE)
Matthew 6.22 'The body gets its light through the eyes. If you have good eyes, all your body will have light. 23 But if your eyes are bad, all your body will be in darkness. If the light in you is dark, it will be very dark for you.'

YOUNG'S LIVING TRANSLATION (YLT)
Matthew 6.22 'The lamp of the body is the eye, if, therefore, thine eye may be perfect, all thy body shall be enlightened, 23 but if thine eye may be evil, all thy body shall be dark; if, therefore, the light that [is] in thee is darkness – the darkness, how great!

EXPANDED BIBLE (EXB)
Matthew 6.22-23 - 22 "The eye is a light [the lamp] for the body. If your eyes are good [healthy; clear], your whole body will be full of light. 23 But if your eyes are·evil

[unhealthy; bad], your whole body will be full of darkness. And if the only light you have [or light you think you have; light in you] is really darkness, then you have the worst darkness [how great that darkness is!].

DISCIPLES' LITERAL NEW TESTAMENT
Matthew 6.22-23 - 22 The lamp of the body is the eye. Therefore if your eye is single, your whole body will be full-of-light. 23 But if your eye is bad, your whole body will be full-of-darkness. If then the light in you is darkness, how great is the darkness!

The passage in Luke 11: 34-36

KJV
Luke 11.34 The light of the body is the eye: therefore when thine eye is single, thy whole body also is full of light; but when thine eye is evil, thy body also is full of darkness.
Luke 11.35 Take heed therefore that the light which is in thee be not darkness.
Luke 11.36 If thy whole body therefore be full of light, having no part dark, the whole shall be full of light, as when the bright shining of a candle doth give thee light.

AMPLIFIED
Luke 11.34 The eye is the lamp of your body. When your eye is clear [spiritually perceptive, focused on God], your whole body also is full of light [benefiting from God's precepts]. But when it is bad [spiritually blind], your body also is full of darkness [devoid of God's word]. 35 Be careful, therefore, that the light that is in you is not darkness. 36 So if your whole body is illuminated, with no dark part, it will be entirely bright [with light], as when the lamp gives you light with its bright rays."

LIVING BIBLE
Luke 11.34 Your eyes light up your inward being. A pure eye lets sunshine into your soul. A lustful eye shuts out the light and plunges you into darkness. 35 So watch out that the sunshine isn't blotted out. 36 If you are filled with light within, with no dark corners, then your face will be radiant too, as though a floodlight is beamed upon you."

THE MESSAGE
Luke 11.33-36 "No one lights a lamp, then hides it in a drawer. It's put on a lamp stand so those entering the room have light to see where they're going. Your eye is a lamp, lighting up your whole body. If you live wide-eyed in wonder and belief, your body fills up with light. If you live squinty-eyed in greed and distrust, your body is a dank cellar. Keep your eyes open, your lamp burning, so you don't get musty and murky. Keep your life as well-lighted as your best-lighted room."

NIRV
Luke 11.34 Your eye is like a lamp for your body. Suppose your eyes are healthy. Then your whole body also is full of light. But suppose your eyes can't see well. Then your body also is full of darkness. 35 So make sure that the light inside you is not darkness. 36 Suppose your whole body is full of light. And suppose no part of it is dark. Then your body will be full of light. It will be just as when a lamp shines its light on you."

NEW LIVING TRANSLATION (NLT)
34 "Your eye is a lamp that provides light for your body. When your eye is good, your whole body is filled with light. But when it is bad, your body is filled with darkness. 35 Make sure that the light you think you have is not actually darkness. 36 If you are filled with light, with no dark corners, then your whole life will be radiant, as though a floodlight were filling you with light."

THE VOICE (VOICE)
33 You need a light to see. Only an idiot would light a lamp and then put it beneath the floor or under a bucket. No, any intelligent person would put the lamp on a table so everyone who comes in the house can see. 34 Listen, your eye, your outlook, the way you see is your lamp. If your way of seeing is functioning well, then your whole life will be enlightened. But if your way of seeing is darkened, then your life will be a dark, dark place. 35 So be careful, people, because your light may be malfunctioning. 36 If your outlook is good, then your whole life will be bright, with no shadowy corners, as when a radiant lamp brightens your home.

WORLDWIDE ENGLISH (NEW TESTAMENT) (WE)
34 Your body gets its light through your eyes. When you have good eyes, all your body has light. But when your eyes are bad, your body is in darkness.

35 So be sure that it is not dark in you where it should be light.

36 If no part of your body is dark, it will all be light. It will be like a lamp that shines to give you light.'

YOUNG'S LITERAL TRANSLATION (YLT)
34 'The lamp of the body is the eye, when then thine eye may be simple, thy whole body also is lightened; and when it may be evil, thy body also is darkened;

35 take heed, then, lest the light that [is] in thee be darkness;

36 if then thy whole body is lightened, not having any part darkened, the whole shall be lightened, as when the lamp by the brightness may give thee light.'

DISCIPLES' LITERAL NEW TESTAMENT
The Lamp Shines So People Can See. Watch Out That Your Eye Can Receive The Light

33 "No one having lit a lamp puts it in a crypt, nor under the basket, but on the lampstand, in order that the ones coming in may see the light. 34 The lamp of the body is your eye. When your eye is single, your whole body is also full-of-light. But when it is bad, your body is also full-of-darkness. 35 So be watching-out that the light in you is not darkness! 36 Therefore if your whole body is full-of-light, not having any part full-of-darkness, [then] the whole body will be full-of-light as when the lamp gives-light-to you with its bright-light."

EXPANDED BIBLE
Be a Light for the World

33 "No one lights a lamp and puts it in a secret place [cellar] or under a bowl [or basket], but on a lampstand so the people who come in can see [the light; Matt. 5:15; Mark 4:21]. 34 Your eye is a light [the lamp] for the body. When your eyes are good [healthy; clear], your whole body will be full of light. But when your eyes are·evil [unhealthy; bad], your whole body will be full of darkness. 35 So be careful·not to let

the light in you become [or that the light in you is not actually] darkness. 36 If your whole body is full of light, and none of it is dark, then you will ·shine bright [be radiant; be filled with light], as when a lamp shines [brightly; with its rays] on you."

CHAPTER 21

HOW TO OVERCOME LUST OF THE EYES AND LUST OF THE FLESH

Galatians 5:16 [This] I say then, Walk in the Spirit, and ye shall not fulfill the lust of the flesh.

Galatians 5:17 For the flesh lusteth against the Spirit, and the Spirit against the flesh: and these are contrary the one to the other: so that ye cannot do the things that ye would.

Galatians 5:18 But if ye be led of the Spirit, ye are not under the law.

Ephesians 4:21 If so be that ye have heard him, and have been taught by him, as the truth is in Jesus:

Ephesians 4:22 That ye put off concerning the former conversation the old man, which is corrupt according to the deceitful lusts;

Ephesians 4:23 And be renewed in the spirit of your mind;

Ephesians 4:24 And that ye put on the new man, which after God is created in righteousness and true holiness.

Ephesians 4:27 Neither give place to the devil.

Ephesians 4:30 And grieve not the holy Spirit of God, whereby ye are sealed unto the day of redemption.

1 Thessalonians 5:22 Abstain from all appearance of evil.

2 Timothy 2:16 But shun profane [and] vain babblings: for they will increase unto more ungodliness.

2 Timothy 2:19 Nevertheless the foundation of God standeth sure, having this seal, The Lord knoweth them that are his. And, Let every one that nameth the name of Christ depart from iniquity.

2 Peter 1:4 Whereby are given unto us exceeding great and precious promises: that by these ye might be partakers of the divine nature, having escaped the corruption that is in the world through lust.

Psalms 119:11 Thy Word have I hid in my heart, that I might not sin against thee.

Psalms 119:9 Wherewithal shall a young man cleanse his way? By taking heed thereto (to his way) according to Thy Word.

(Amplified version) By taking heed and keeping watch on himself according to your word, conforming his life to it.

WHAT TO DO

Hebrews 12:1 Wherefore seeing we also are compassed about with so great a cloud of witnesses, let us lay aside every weight, and the sin which doth so easily beset [us], and let us run with patience the race that is set before us,

Hebrews 12:4 Ye have not yet resisted unto blood, striving against sin.

Hebrews 12:14 <u>Follow</u> peace with all [men], and <u>holiness</u>, without which <u>no man shall see the Lord</u>:

James 1:27 Pure religion and undefiled before God and the Father is this, To visit the fatherless and widows in their affliction, [and] to <u>keep himself unspotted</u> from the world.

James 4:1 From whence [come] wars and fightings among you? [come they] not hence, [even] of your <u>lusts</u> that war in your members?

James 4:2 Ye <u>lust</u>, and have not: ye kill, and desire to have, and cannot obtain: ye fight and war, yet ye have not, because ye ask not.

James 4:7 <u>Submit</u> yourselves therefore to God. <u>Resist</u> the devil, and he will flee from you.

James 4:8 <u>Draw nigh</u> to God, and he will draw nigh to you. Cleanse [your] hands, [ye] sinners; and purify [your] hearts, [ye] <u>double minded</u>.

1 Peter 1:14 As obedient children, not fashioning yourselves according to the former <u>lusts</u> in your ignorance:

1 Peter 1:15 But as he which hath called you is holy, so be ye <u>holy</u> in all manner of conversation;

1 Peter 1:16 Because it is written, <u>Be ye holy</u>; for I am holy.

1 Peter 2:11 Dearly beloved, I beseech [you] as strangers and pilgrims, <u>abstain from fleshly lusts</u>, which <u>war against the soul</u>;

1 Peter 5:8 Be sober, be vigilant; because your adversary the devil, as a roaring lion, walketh about, seeking whom he <u>may</u> devour:

1 Peter 5:9 Whom <u>resist</u> stedfast in the faith, knowing that the same afflictions are accomplished in your brethren that are in the world.

Romans 13:14 But put ye on the Lord Jesus Christ, and make not provision for the flesh, to fulfill the <u>lusts</u> thereof.

2 Corinthians 10:5 <u>Casting down</u> imaginations, and every high thing that exalts itself against the knowledge of God, and <u>bringing into captivity</u> every <u>thought</u> to the obedience of Christ.

Philippians 4:8 Only think on those things that are true, honest, just, pure, holy, lovely, good report, virtuous, praiseworthy.

Hebrews 9:14 How much more shall the <u>blood of Christ purge</u> and cleanse your <u>mind</u> from dead, evil <u>thoughts</u> to serve the living God.

1 John 2:15 Love not the world, neither the things that are in the world. If any man love the world, the love of the Father is not in him.

1 John 2:16 For all that is in the world, the <u>lust</u> of the flesh [craving for sensual gratification], and the <u>lust</u> of the eyes [greedy longings of the mind] and the pride of life [assurance in one's own resources or in the stability of earthly things] is not of the Father, but is of the world.

HOW TEMPTATION WORKS

James 1:14 But every man is tempted, when he is drawn away of <u>his own</u> lust, and enticed.

James 1:15 Then when lust hath conceived, it bringeth forth sin: and sin, when it is finished, bringeth forth death.

(When I yield and give way to the temptation to lust, my own lust conceives and gives birth to sin.)

Genesis 4:6 And the LORD said unto Cain, Why art thou wroth? and why is thy countenance fallen?

Genesis 4:7 If thou doest well, shalt thou not be accepted? and if thou doest not well, sin lieth at the door. And unto thee [shall be] his desire, and thou shalt rule over him.

Genesis 4:6-7 (New Jerusalem Bible) Yahweh asked Cain, "Why are you angry and downcast? If you are well disposed, ought you not to lift up your head? But if you are ill disposed, is not sin at the door like a crouching beast hungering for you, which you must master?

GUARD YOUR EYES

Psalms 119:105 Thy Word is a Lamp unto my feet, and a Light unto my path.

130 The entrance of thy words gives light; it gives understanding unto the simple.

Luke 11:34-36 **(Amp)** Your eye is the lamp of your body; when your eye is sound and fulfilling its office, your whole body is full of light; but when it is not sound and is not fulfilling its office, your body is full of darkness.

35 Be careful therefore that the light that is in you be not darkness.

36 If your entire body is illuminated, having no part dark, it will be wholly bright [with light], as when a lamp with its bright rays gives you light.

(Living Bible) Luke 11:34-36 Your eye lights up your inward being. A pure eye lets sunshine into your soul. A lustful eye shuts out the light and plunges you into darkness.

35 So watch out that the sunshine isn't blotted out.

36 If you are filled with light within, with no dark corners, then the outside will be radiant too, as though a floodlight is beamed upon you.

Job 31:1 I dictated a covenant - an agreement - to my eyes; how then could I look [lustfully] upon a girl?

1 John 1:7 But if we walk in the light, as He is in the light, we have fellowship one with another, and the blood of Jesus Christ His Son cleanses us from all sin.

Matthew 6:22 The light of the body is the eye: if therefore thine eye be single, thy whole body shall be full of light.

Matthew 6:23 But if thine eye be evil, thy whole body shall be full of darkness. If therefore the light that is in thee be darkness, how great is that darkness!

BEWARE OF LUSTING AFTER WOMEN (OR MEN)

Proverbs 6:23-25 For the commandment is a lamp; and the law is light, and reproofs of instruction are the way of life:

24 To keep thee from the evil woman, from the flattery of the tongue of a strange woman.

25 Lust not after her beauty in thine heart, neither let her take thee with her eyelids.

Proverbs 6:26 For by means of a whorish woman a man is brought to a piece of bread: and the adulteress will hunt for the precious life.

Proverbs 6:32 But whoso committeth adultery with a woman lacks understanding; he that does it destroys his own soul.

Matthew 5:28-29 Whosoever looketh on a woman to lust after her has committed adultery with her already in his heart.

29 And if thy right eye <u>offend</u> thee, <u>pluck it out</u>, and cast it from thee: for it is <u>profitable for thee</u> that one of thy members should perish, and not that thy whole body should be cast into hell.

   The second look is sin.

"Whosoever <u>looketh</u>" - not accidental sight but an intentional viewing the object. More than a passing glance, but a lingering view.

"<u>Lust</u>" - is uncontrolled desire that cannot be satisfied. Inner attitudes lead to outward actions. Sin lives in the will. Thoughts need to be in subjection.

"<u>If eye offend thee</u>" - not displease, but hinders, interferes, and causes you to stumble. All occasions of sin must be relinquished.

1 Thessalonians 5:22 Abstain from all appearances of evil.

"<u>Pluck it out</u>" - Divine surgery for health and life. Action required; rigidly restrain or strictly govern and control. Rigidly restrain your eye. Pluck eye out of sinful situation. That which is the cause of sin is to be given up as the sin itself.

The single eye: Matthew 5:22-23, Luke 11:34. The activities of the body are directed according to the light received. Light is having God's point of view. If your eye is pure then there will be sunshine in your soul. Just as the physical eye is the receptacle of light, the spiritual eye is the receptacle of God's Word. No double vision. Evil eye is darkness. The physical condition is figurative of the moral. Singleness of purpose keeps us from the snare of having a double treasure and consequently a divided heart.

Outcome = "<u>Profitable for thee</u>" - an open door leads to more problems and attacks. Insures harmony, be in tune, useable now for the Lord. Guard your gates!

2 Timothy 2:21 If a man therefore purge himself from these, he shall be a vessel unto honor, sanctified, and meet (fit) for the Master's use, and prepared unto every good work.

2 Timothy 2:22 Flee also youthful lusts: but follow righteousness, faith, charity, peace, with them that call on the Lord out of a pure heart.

<u>Why your Life is Unfruitful: Living in a Spiritual Briar Patch</u>

Mark 4:18 And these are they which are sown among thorns: such as hear the word,
19 And the cares of this world, and the deceitfulness of riches, and the lusts of other things entering in, choke the Word, and it becometh unfruitful.

1 Thessalonians 4:3 For this is the will of God, even your sanctification, that you should abstain from fornication:

1 Thessalonians 4:4 That every one of you should know how to possess his vessel in sanctification and honor.

1 Thessalonians 4:5 Not in the lust of concupiscence…(this word means a strong sexual longing, especially for what is forbidden)

1 Thessalonians 4:7 For God has not called us unto uncleanness, but unto holiness.

1 Thessalonians 4:8 **(Amp)** Therefore whoever disregards, sets aside and rejects this, disregards not man but God, Whose very Spirit Whom He gives to you is holy, chaste, pure.

John 5:14 "Sin no more, lest a worst thing come upon you." – Jesus Christ

CHAPTER 22

I HAVE POWER OVER SIN AND ADDICTION

Read This Out Loud during the Day and at Bedtime to Be Set Free!
Place the Helmet of Salvation over Your Mind to Prevent Bad Dreams.

I have power and authority over temptation and addictions. Luke 10:19
I must realize that the urge to _(name of sin/addiction)_ is merely a temptation. That urge is a compulsion. If I feel compelled to _____, I realize it is a bait of satan, it is a lure to get me to fall down the slippery slope of sin.

Jesus gave me power over satan, sin and temptation. How? Through His Word and His Blood! The Word of God is Jesus! The Word is in me. He that is in me is greater than he that is in the world. 1 John 4:4

Being tempted, compelled and urged to _____ is a sin if you give in to that urge. Fight that urge with the Word. The key to overcoming fleshly, carnal urges is using the Word, the scriptures, quoting the Word of God out loud. Verbally cast down the thoughts, daydreams, and imaginations compelling and tempting you.

Obsessive-compulsive behavior is in the mind. I can control my hands because I don't permit my fists to give me a black eye. In the same way, I have power over my mind just as I have power over my hands. I DO cast down compulsive thoughts in the name of Jesus. Get out of my mind, demon thoughts! The Word of God says:

"Casting down imaginations and every high thing that exalts itself against the knowledge of God, and bringing into captivity every thought to the obedience of Christ." 2 Corinthians 10:5

I cast down thoughts that are urging me to _____. I am using the Sword of the Spirit against you, satan. You demon thoughts are exalting yourself. You are acting as an arrogant bully against the Word of God, and the more powerful knowledge of God in me.

I place you demon thoughts under arrest in the name of Jesus Christ, the Almighty God. I place under arrest and bring into captivity every demon thought urging me to ____ and ____ to the obedience of Christ. By an act of my mind and willpower I will obey Jesus Christ. I will obey the Word of God.

In John 14 Jesus says, "If you love Me, you will obey Me. If you disobey Me, you don't truly love Me."

I will obey Jesus. I will obey the Word of God. I am an overcomer. I am sin-free. I am addiction-free! I can and do cast down temptations. I can and do cast down evil urges and obsessive compulsions. I can and do cast down all urges to _____, because "I can do all things through Christ who strengthens me." Philippians 4:13

My mind is pure, holy, undefiled, and restored. I only think on things that are true, honest, just, pure, lovely, good report, virtuous and praiseworthy. Philippians 4:8

I choose to serve only one Master! I don't serve mammon or lust. Matthew 6:24
Jesus loves me. Jesus is pulling for me and encouraging me. Jesus is on my side! If God is for me, who can be against me? God plus me is a majority! Jesus is the Word of God as it says in John 1:1. Jesus is strengthening me against temptation.

I will sin no more lest a worse thing come upon me. John 5:14

I will renew my mind in the areas of my weakness. Romans 12:2

I will use the word of God as a hammer to break down the strongholds in my life. Jeremiah 23:29

CHAPTER 23

ROMANS 6 FROM LIVING NEW TESTAMENT

This chapter has been personalized to be in the first person tense. Read it <u>out loud</u> to persuade yourself of the reality of God's Word. Make it personal to you and your life.

1 Well then, shall I keep on sinning so that God can keep on showing me more and more kindness and forgiveness?

2,3 Of course not! Should I keep on sinning when I don't have to? For sin's power over me was broken when I became a Christian and was baptized to become a part of Jesus Christ; through His death the power of my sinful nature was shattered.

4 My old sin-loving nature was buried with Him by baptism when He died, and when God the Father, with glorious power, brought Him back to life again, I was given His wonderful new life to enjoy.

5 For I have become a part of Him, and so I died with Him, so to speak, when He died; and now I share His new life and shall rise as He did.

6 My old evil desires were nailed to the cross with Him; that part of me that loves to sin was crushed and fatally wounded, so that my sin-loving body is no longer under sin's control, no longer needs to be a slave to sin;

7 For when I am deadened to sin I am freed from all its allure and its power over me.

8 And since my old sin-loving nature "died" with Christ, I know that I will share His new life.

9 Christ rose from the dead and will never die again. Death no longer has any power over Him.

10 He died once for all to end sin's power, but now He lives forever in unbroken fellowship with God.

11 So I look upon my old sin nature as dead and unresponsive to sin; I am alive to God, alert to Him, through Jesus Christ our Lord.

12 I will not let sin control my puny body any longer; I do not give in to its sinful desires.

13 I do not let any part of my body become a tool of wickedness, to be used for sinning; but I give myself completely to God – every part of me – for I am back from death and I want to be a tool in the hands of God, to be used for His good purposes.

14 Sin need never again be my master, for now I am no longer tied to the law where sin enslaves me, but I am free under God's favor and mercy.

15 Does this mean that I can go ahead and sin and not worry about it? (For my salvation does not depend on keeping the law, but on receiving God's grace!) Of course not!

16 I realize that I can choose my own master. I can choose sin (with death) or else obedience (with acquittal). The one to whom I offer myself – he will take me and be my master and I will be his slave.

17 Thank God that though I once chose to be a slave of sin, I have obeyed with all my heart the teaching to which God has committed to me.

18 And now I am free from my old master, sin; and I have become a slave to my new master, righteousness.

19 I speak this way, using the illustration of slaves and masters because it is easy to understand: just as I used to be slave to all kinds of sin, so now I must let myself be slave to all that is right and holy.

20 In those days when I was a slave of sin I didn't bother much with goodness.

21 And what was the result? Evidently not good, since I am ashamed now even to think about those things I used to do, for all of them end in eternal doom.

22 But now I am free from the power of sin and am a slave of God, and His benefits to me include holiness and everlasting life.

23 For the wages of sin is death, but the free gift of God is eternal life through Jesus Christ my Lord.

CHAPTER 24

SCRIPTURES ON HOW TO STOP SINNING

Matthew 6.24 No man can serve two masters: for either he will hate the one and love the other; or else he will hold to the one and despise the other. Ye cannot serve God and mammon.

John 5.14 Afterward Jesus findeth him in the temple, and said unto him, Behold, thou art made whole: sin no more, lest a worse thing come unto thee.

John 8.11 She said, No man, Lord. And Jesus said unto her, Neither do I condemn thee: go, and sin no more.

Matthew 7.21-23 Not every one that saith unto me, Lord, Lord, shall enter into the kingdom of heaven; but he that doeth the will of my Father which is in heaven.

22 Many will say to me in that day, Lord, Lord, have we not prophesied in thy name? and in thy name have cast out devils? and in thy name done many wonderful works?

23 And then will I profess unto them, I never knew you: depart from me, ye that work iniquity.

Ezek 33.31-32 And they come unto thee as the people cometh, and they sit before thee [as] my people, and they hear thy words, but they will not do them: for with their mouth they shew much love, [but] their heart goeth after their covetousness.

32 And, lo, thou [art] unto them as a very lovely song of one that hath a pleasant voice, and can play well on an instrument: for they hear thy words, but they do them not.

Mark 7.6 He answered and said unto them, Well hath Esaias prophesied of you hypocrites, as it is written, This people honoureth me with [their] lips, but their heart is far from me.

Luke 6.46-49 And why call ye me, Lord, Lord, and do not the things which I say?

47 Whosoever cometh to me, and heareth my sayings, and doeth them, I will shew you to whom he is like:

48 He is like a man which built an house, and digged deep, and laid the foundation on a rock: and when the flood arose, the stream beat vehemently upon that house, and could not shake it: for it was founded upon a rock.

49 But he that heareth, and doeth not, is like a man that without a foundation built an house upon the earth; against which the stream did beat vehemently, and immediately it fell; and the ruin of that house was great.

Titus 1.15-16 Unto the pure all things [are] pure: but unto them that are defiled and unbelieving [is] nothing pure; but even their mind and conscience is defiled.
16 They profess that they know God; but in works they deny [him], being abominable, and disobedient, and unto every good work reprobate.

1 John 3.18-24 My little children, let us not love in word, neither in tongue; but in deed and in truth.
19 And hereby we know that we are of the truth, and shall assure our hearts before him.
20 For if our heart condemn us, God is greater than our heart, and knoweth all things.
21 Beloved, if our heart condemn us not, [then] have we confidence toward God.
22 And whatsoever we ask, we receive of him, because we keep his commandments, and do those things that are pleasing in his sight.
23 And this is his commandment, That we should believe on the name of his Son Jesus Christ, and love one another, as he gave us commandment.
24 And he that keepeth his commandments dwelleth in him, and he in him. And hereby we know that he abideth in us, by the Spirit which he hath given us.

Isaiah 1.16 Wash you, make you clean; put away the evil of your doings from before mine eyes; cease to do evil;

Romans 6.12-14, 16, 22 Let not sin therefore reign in your mortal body, that ye should obey it in the lusts thereof.
13 Neither yield ye your members [as] instruments of unrighteousness unto sin: but yield yourselves unto God, as those that are alive from the dead, and your members [as] instruments of righteousness unto God.
14 For sin shall not have dominion over you: for ye are not under the law, but under grace.
16 Know ye not, that to whom ye yield yourselves servants to obey, his servants ye are to whom ye obey; whether of sin unto death, or of obedience unto righteousness?
22 But now being made free from sin, and become servants to God, ye have your fruit unto holiness, and the end everlasting life.

CHAPTER 25

TRANSFIGURATION SCRIPTURES
REVEALING THE ORIGINAL NATURE OF JESUS

Matthew 17.2-9 And was transfigured before them: and his face did shine as the sun, and his raiment was white as the light.
3 And, behold, there appeared unto them Moses and Elias talking with him.
4 Then answered Peter, and said unto Jesus, Lord, it is good for us to be here: if thou wilt, let us make here three tabernacles; one for thee, and one for Moses, and one for Elias.

5 While he yet spake, behold, a bright cloud overshadowed them: and behold a voice out of the cloud, which said, This is my beloved Son, in whom I am well pleased; hear ye him.

6 And when the disciples heard it, they fell on their face, and were sore afraid.

7 And Jesus came and touched them, and said, Arise, and be not afraid.

8 And when they had lifted up their eyes, they saw no man, save Jesus only.

9 And as they came down from the mountain, Jesus charged them, saying, Tell the vision to no man, until the Son of man be risen again from the dead.

Mark 9.2-8 And after six days Jesus taketh with him Peter, and James, and John, and leadeth them up into an high mountain apart by themselves: and he was transfigured before them.

Mark 9:3 And his raiment became shining, exceeding white as snow; so as no fuller on earth can white them.

Mark 9:4 And there appeared unto them Elias with Moses: and they were talking with Jesus.

Mark 9:5 And Peter answered and said to Jesus, Master, it is good for us to be here: and let us make three tabernacles; one for thee, and one for Moses, and one for Elias.

Mark 9:6 For he wist not what to say; for they were sore afraid.

Mark 9:7 And there was a cloud that overshadowed them: and a voice came out of the cloud, saying, This is my beloved Son: hear him.

Mark 9:8 And suddenly, when they had looked round about, they saw no man any more, save Jesus only with themselves.

Luke 9.28-36 And it came to pass about an eight days after these sayings, he took Peter and John and James, and went up into a mountain to pray.

29 And as he prayed, the fashion of his countenance was altered, and his raiment was white and glistering.

30 And, behold, there talked with him two men, which were Moses and Elias:

31 Who appeared in glory, and spake of his decease which he should accomplish at Jerusalem.

32 But Peter and they that were with him were heavy with sleep: and when they were awake, they saw his glory, and the two men that stood with him.

9.33 And it came to pass, as they departed from him, Peter said unto Jesus, Master, it is good for us to be here: and let us make three tabernacles; one for thee, and one for Moses, and one for Elias: not knowing what he said.

34 While he thus spake, there came a cloud, and overshadowed them: and they feared as they entered into the cloud.

35 And there came a voice out of the cloud, saying, This is my beloved Son: hear him.

36 And when the voice was past, Jesus was found alone. And they kept it close, and told no man in those days any of those things which they had seen.

2 Peter 1:16–18

2 Peter 1:16 For we have not followed cunningly devised fables, when we made known unto you the power and coming of our Lord Jesus Christ, but were eyewitnesses of his majesty.

2 Peter 1:17 For he received from God the Father honour and glory, when there came such a voice to him from the excellent glory, This is my beloved Son, in whom I am well pleased.

2 Peter 1:18 And this voice which came from heaven we heard, when we were with him in the holy mount.

Summary of Every Instance

… his face did shine as the sun, and his raiment was white as the light.

… he was transfigured before them.

Mark 9:3 And his raiment became shining, exceeding white as snow; so as no fuller on earth can white them.

the fashion of his countenance was altered, and his raiment was white and glistering.

Moses and Elias: Who appeared in glory,

they saw His glory,

there came a cloud, and overshadowed them: and they feared as they entered into the cloud.

Luke 9:35 And there came a voice out of the cloud, saying, This is my beloved Son: hear him.

2 Peter 1.16 but were eyewitnesses of his majesty.

2 Peter 1:17 For he received from God the Father honour and glory, when there came such a voice to him from the excellent glory, This is my beloved Son, in whom I am well pleased.

CHAPTER 26

JESUS PAID FOR YOUR HEALING ON THE CROSS

Romans 8:11 But if the Spirit of him that raised up Jesus from the dead dwell in you, he that raised up Christ from the dead shall also quicken (enliven, give vitality to) your mortal bodies by his Spirit that dwelleth in you.

WHAT JESUS WENT THROUGH FOR YOU

Crown of thorns hammered into his head= healing of your mind, willpower, emotions.

Lashes from the scourging whip caused stripes and a torn back. By those stripes you were healed.

Jesus was Holiest of all = being totally naked on the cross paid for your freedom from shame.

He endured mocking, verbal and physical abuse = this redeemed you from mockery and bullying.

His hands were nailed to the tree = to redeem, purify, sanctify and bless the work of your hands.

His feet were nailed to the tree = to redeem your walk, direction, goals, path of life.

He was nailed to a tree= He is the tree of Life; we are redeemed from the effects of eating from the tree of the knowledge of good and evil.

The fall of man started in the Garden of Eden. The eternal life of man started in the garden of Gethsemane.

Priests sacrificed lambs in Old Testament = Jesus is our High Priest, He is the Lamb of God, the last Adam, the final and only sin offering that pleases Father God.

HEALING SCRIPTURES AND CONFESSIONS

Your complete healing and divine health was paid for by Jesus Christ. When Jesus was crucified on the cross, that was a sin offering to God the Father that paid the price for our complete healing from mental, emotional and physical sickness and disease. Our entire bundle of healing, salvation and deliverance from poverty, bondage and oppression was all paid for by Jesus on the cross of Calvary. Jesus yelled out before dying, "It is finished." That literally means the price to ransom you from the devil's bondage was "PAID IN FULL." Your entire bundle plan of redemption was paid in full. It is up to YOU to receive it and claim it for yourself.

Isaiah 52:14 <u>Amplified Bible</u>: For many the Servant of God became an object of horror; many were astonished. His face and His whole appearance were marred more than any man's, and His form beyond that of the sons of men.
Isaiah 53:4 Surely He has borne our griefs – sickness, weakness and distress – and carried our sorrows and pain of punishment. Yet we ignorantly considered Him stricken, smitten and afflicted by God as if with leprosy.
Isaiah 53:5 But He was wounded for our transgressions, He was bruised for our guilt and iniquities; the chastisement needful to obtain peace and well-being for us was upon Him, and with the stripes that wounded Him we are healed and made whole
Matthew 27:30 And they spit upon him, and took the reed, and smote him on the head. (Jesus was wearing the crown of thorns. Being hit on the head drove the thorns in deeper; this is a sign of being redeemed from mental and emotional torment and mental illness. Jesus bore the torment so we don't have to.)

1 Peter 2:24 Who his own self bore our sins in his own body on the tree, that we, being dead to sins, should live unto righteousness: by whose stripes <u>you were healed</u>.
Psalms 107:20 He sent his word, and <u>healed</u> them, and delivered them from their destructions.

Jesus bore my sins in His Body on the tree (the cross.) Because He did this for me, I am dead to sin and alive unto God and by His stripes I am healed and made whole. Jesus bore my sickness and carried my pains. Therefore, I give no place to sickness or pain. For God sent His Word and healed me. The Divine Life of First Peter 2:24 is a reality in my flesh. This word is restoring every cell of my body.

1 John 4:4 You are of God, little children, and have overcome them: because greater is he that is in you, than he that is in the world.

Revelation 12:11 And they overcame him (the devil) by the blood of the Lamb, and by the word of their testimony; and they loved not their lives unto the death.

Father, because of your word I am an overcomer. I overcome the world, the flesh and the devil, by the Blood of the Lamb, the bloody stripes of Jesus, and the word of my testimony.

John 10:10 The thief (the devil) comes not, but for to steal, and to kill, and to destroy: I am come that they might have life, and that they might have <u>life more abundantly</u>.

John 6:63 It is the Spirit that quickens (makes alive); the flesh profits nothing: the words that I speak unto you, they are Spirit, and they are life.

You have given me abundant life. I receive that life through Your Word. Divine Life flows to every organ of my body bringing Divine healing and health.

Proverbs 4:20-22 My son, attend to my words; incline your ear unto my sayings. Let them not depart from your eyes; keep them in the midst of your heart. For they are life unto those that find them, and health to all their flesh.

Heavenly Father, I treasure Your Word. I incline my ears to your sayings. I will not let your words depart from my eyes. I keep them in the center of my heart. Your words are Divine LIFE and Divine healing to all my spirit, soul and body, and to my mind, will, heart and emotions.

Deuteronomy 34:7 Moses was 120 years old when he died: his eyes were not dim, nor was his natural force (strength) abated (weakened.)

As God was with Moses, so is He with me. My eyes are not dim, neither are my natural forces weakened. Blessed are my eyes for they see and my ears, for they hear.

Psalms 91:10-11 There shall no evil befall you, neither shall any plague come near your dwelling. For he shall give his angels charge over you, to keep you in all your ways.

No evil will befall me, neither shall any plague come near my dwelling. For You have given your angels charge over me. They keep me in all my ways. Life, healing and health is mine.

Matthew 8:17 That it might be fulfilled which was spoken by Isaiah the prophet, saying, Himself took our infirmities, and bare our sicknesses.

Jesus took my infirmities and bore my sicknesses. Because He did this for me, I refuse to allow sickness to have dominion over my body.

Galatians 3:13 Christ has redeemed us from the curse of the law, being made a curse for us: for it is written, Cursed is every one that hangs on a tree:

I am redeemed from the curse. This healing word is flowing in my blood stream. It flows to every cell of my body, restoring life and health.

I DECREE HEALING

Divine life is in the creative power of my tongue! I decree and send forth to my entire body DIVINE HEALING, DIVINE HEALTH, DIVINE LIFE, and CREATIVE RESTORATION to happen NOW in the name of Jesus!

Luke 1:37 The angel Gabriel told Mary: "For with God nothing will be impossible."
Luke 1.38 Mary responded: "Let it be to me according to your word."

Isaiah 53.5 But Jesus was wounded for our transgressions, he was bruised for our iniquities: the chastisement of our peace was upon him; and with his stripes we are healed.
"May it be done to me according to your word." HCSB version
1 Peter 2.24 Who his own self bare our sins in his own body on the tree, that we, being dead to sins, should live unto righteousness: by whose stripes ye were healed.
"Let this happen to me according to your word." NET version
We should follow Mary's example. Every time we read a promise from God, we should say what Mary said. "Let this promise from God be manifested in my life according to Your Word!"

CHAPTER 27

HEALING OF FEET

2 Samuel 22:34 He maketh my feet like <u>hinds' feet</u>: and setteth me upon my high places. (A hind is a deer.)

2 Chronicles 16:12-13 And Asa in the thirty and ninth year of his reign was diseased in his <u>feet</u>, until his disease was exceeding great: yet in his disease he sought not to the LORD, but to the physicians.
13 And Asa slept with his fathers, and died in the one and fortieth year of his reign.

Acts 3:6-8 Then Peter said, Silver and gold have I none; but such as I have give I thee: In the name of Jesus Christ of Nazareth rise up and walk.
7 And he took him by the right hand, and lifted him up: and immediately his <u>feet and ankle bones</u> received strength.
8 And he <u>leaping up stood, and walked</u>, and entered with them into the temple, <u>walking, and leaping</u>, and praising God.

Acts 14:8-10 And there sat a certain man at Lystra, <u>impotent in his feet</u>, being a cripple from his mother's womb, who never had walked:
9 The same heard Paul speak: who stedfastly beholding him, and perceiving that he had faith to be healed,
10 Said with a loud voice, Stand upright on thy feet. And he <u>leaped and walked</u>.

Romans 10:15 And how shall they preach, except they be sent? as it is written, How beautiful are the <u>feet</u> of them that preach the gospel of peace, and bring glad tidings of good things!

Ephesians 6:15 And your <u>feet</u> shod with the preparation of the gospel of peace;

CHAPTER 28

HEALING THE WOUNDED SPIRIT

God knew us from the womb. Here are Scriptures to meditate on for healing a broken heart and a wounded spirit.

The spirit of man

Job 32:8 But [there is] a <u>spirit</u> in man: and the inspiration of the Almighty giveth them understanding.

Psalms 51:17 The sacrifices of God [are] a broken <u>spirit</u>: a broken and a contrite heart, O God, thou wilt not despise.

Proverbs 15:4 A wholesome tongue [is] a tree of life: but perverseness therein [is] a breach in the <u>spirit</u>.

Proverbs 15:13 A merry heart maketh a cheerful countenance: but by sorrow of the heart the <u>spirit</u> is broken.

Proverbs 16:32 [He that is] slow to anger [is] better than the mighty; and he that ruleth his <u>spirit</u> than he that taketh a city.

Proverbs 17:22 A merry heart doeth good [like] a medicine: but a broken <u>spirit</u> drieth the bones.

Proverbs 18:14 The <u>spirit</u> of a man will sustain his infirmity; but a wounded <u>spirit</u> who can bear?

Proverbs 20:27 The <u>spirit</u> of man [is] the candle of the LORD, searching all the inward parts of the belly.

Proverbs 25:28 He that [hath] no rule over his own <u>spirit</u> [is like] a city [that is] broken down, [and] without walls.

Ecclesiates 11:5 As thou knowest not what [is] the way of the <u>spirit</u>, [nor] how the bones [do grow] in the womb of her that is with child: even so thou knowest not the works of God who maketh all.

Ecclesiastes 12:7 Then shall the dust return to the earth as it was: and the <u>spirit</u> shall return unto God who gave it.

Isaiah 61:1-3 (KJV) The Spirit of the Lord GOD [is] upon me; because the LORD hath anointed me to preach good tidings unto the meek (poor); he hath sent me to bind up (heal) the <u>brokenhearted</u>, to proclaim liberty to the captives, and the opening of the prison to [them that are] bound;

2 To proclaim the acceptable year of the LORD, and the day of vengeance of our God; to comfort all that mourn;

3 To appoint unto (console) them that mourn in Zion, to give unto them beauty for ashes, the oil of joy for mourning, the garment of praise for the spirit of heaviness; that they

might be called trees of righteousness, the planting of the LORD, that he might be glorified.

Luke 4:18 The Spirit of the Lord [is] upon me, because he hath anointed me to preach the gospel to the poor; he hath sent me to heal the brokenhearted, to preach deliverance to the captives, and recovering of sight to the blind, to set at liberty them that are bruised,

Zechariah 12:1 The burden of the word of the LORD for Israel, saith the LORD, which stretcheth forth the heavens, and layeth the foundation of the earth, and formeth the spirit of man within him.

John 4:23 But the hour cometh, and now is, when the true worshippers shall worship the Father in spirit and in truth: for the Father seeketh such to worship him.

Romans 8:16 The Spirit itself beareth witness with our spirit, that we are the children of God:

Romans 11:8 (According as it is written, God hath given them the spirit of slumber, eyes that they should not see, and ears that they should not hear;) unto this day.

1 Corinthians 2:11 For what man knoweth the things of a man, save the spirit of man which is in him? even so the things of God knoweth no man, but the Spirit of God.

1 Corinthians 6:20 For ye are bought with a price: therefore glorify God in your body, and in your spirit, which are God's.

1 Corinthians 14:14 For if I pray in an [unknown] tongue, my spirit prayeth, but my understanding is unfruitful.

1 Corinthians 15:45 And so it is written, The first man Adam was made a living soul; the last Adam [was made] a quickening spirit.

Ephesians 3:16-17 That he would grant you, according to the riches of his glory, to be strengthened with might by his Spirit in the inner man; That Christ may dwell in your hearts by faith; that ye, being rooted and grounded in love,

Ephesians 4:23 And be renewed in the spirit of your mind;

1 Thessalonians 5:23 And the very God of peace sanctify you wholly; and [I pray God] your whole spirit and soul and body be preserved blameless unto the coming of our Lord Jesus Christ.

Broken Heart

Psalms 34:18 The LORD [is] nigh unto them that are of a broken heart; and saveth such as be of a contrite spirit.

Psalms 147:3 He healeth the broken in heart, and bindeth up their wounds.

God knew us from the womb

Job 31:15 Did not he that made me in the womb make him? and did not one fashion us in the womb?

Psalms 22:9-10 But thou [art] he that took me out of the womb: thou didst make me hope [when I was] upon my mother's breasts. I was cast upon thee from the womb: thou [art] my God from my mother's belly.

Psalms 139:13-17 For thou hast possessed my reins: thou hast covered me in my mother's womb.

14 I will praise thee; for I am fearfully [and] wonderfully made: marvellous [are] thy works; and [that] my soul knoweth right well.

15 My substance was not hid from thee, when I was made in secret, [and] curiously wrought in the lowest parts of the earth.
16 Thine eyes did see my substance, yet being unperfect; and in thy book all [my members] were written, [which] in continuance were fashioned, when [as yet there was] none of them.
17 How precious also are thy thoughts unto me, O God! how great is the sum of them!
Psalms 71:6 By thee have I been holden up from the womb: thou art he that took me out of my mother's bowels: my praise [shall be] continually of thee.
Isaiah 44:24 Thus saith the LORD, thy redeemer, and he that formed thee from the womb, I [am] the LORD that maketh all [things]; that stretcheth forth the heavens alone; that spreadeth abroad the earth by myself;
Isaiah 46:3-4 Hearken unto me, O house of Jacob, and all the remnant of the house of Israel, which are borne [by me] from the belly, which are carried from the womb:
46:4 And [even] to [your] old age I [am] he; and [even] to hoar hairs will I carry [you]: I have made, and I will bear; even I will carry, and will deliver [you].
Jeremiah 1:5 Before I formed thee in the belly I knew thee; and before thou camest forth out of the womb I sanctified thee, [and] I ordained thee a prophet unto the nations.
Jeremiah 20:17-18 Because he slew me not from the womb; or that my mother might have been my grave, and her womb [to be] always great [with me].
18 Wherefore came I forth out of the womb to see labour and sorrow, that my days should be consumed with shame?
Luke 1:41 And it came to pass, that, when Elisabeth heard the salutation of Mary, the babe leaped in her womb; and Elisabeth was filled with the Holy Ghost:

CHAPTER 29

RESTORING THE CARNAL MIND

Genesis 3:13 And Jehovah God saith to the woman, "What is this thou hast done?" And the woman saith, 'The serpent hath caused me to forget – and I do eat.' "The serpent deceived me, beguiled me..." The word for beguiled means caused me to forget. Has the devil ever caused you to forget something was sin?

Put on your spiritual armor

Ephesians 6: 10-18
10 Finally, my brethren, be strong in the Lord, and in the power of his might.
11 Put on the whole armour of God, that ye may be able to stand against the wiles of the devil.
12 For we wrestle not against flesh and blood, but against principalities, against powers, against the rulers of the darkness of this world, against spiritual wickedness in high [places].
13 Wherefore take unto you the whole armour of God, that ye may be able to withstand in the evil day, and having done all, to stand.
14 Stand therefore, having your loins girt about with truth, and having on the breastplate of righteousness;
15 And your feet shod with the preparation of the gospel of peace;

16 Above all, taking the shield of faith, wherewith ye shall be able to quench all the fiery darts of the wicked.

17 And take the helmet of salvation, and the sword of the Spirit, which is the word of God:

18 Praying always with all prayer and supplication in the Spirit, and watching thereunto with all perseverance and supplication for all saints;

Cast down imaginations and bring bad thoughts into captivity

Memorize 2 Corinthians 10: 3-5

3 For though we walk in the flesh, we do not war after the flesh:

4 For the weapons of our warfare [are] not carnal, but mighty through God to the pulling down of strong holds;

5 Casting down imaginations, and every high thing that exalteth itself against the knowledge of God, and bringing into captivity every thought to the obedience of Christ;

The Word "Mind" in STRONGS CONCORDANCE

Matthew 22.37 Jesus said unto him, Thou shalt love the Lord thy God with all thy heart, and with all thy soul, and with all thy <u>mind</u>.

Mark 5.15 And they come to Jesus, and see him that was possessed with the devil, and had the legion, sitting, and clothed, and in his right <u>mind</u>: and they were afraid.

Romans 1.28-32 And even as they did not like to retain God in [their] knowledge, God gave them over to a reprobate <u>mind</u>, to do those things which are not convenient;

29 Being filled with all unrighteousness, fornication, wickedness, covetousness, maliciousness; full of envy, murder, debate, deceit, malignity; whisperers,

30 Backbiters, haters of God, despiteful, proud, boasters, inventors of evil things, disobedient to parents,

31 Without understanding, covenant breakers, without natural affection, implacable, unmerciful:

32 Who knowing the judgment of God, that they which commit such things are worthy of death, not only do the same, but have pleasure in them that do them.

Romans 7.23 But I see another law in my members, warring against the law of my <u>mind</u>, and bringing me into captivity to the law of sin which is in my members.

Romans 7.25 I thank God through Jesus Christ our Lord. So then with the <u>mind</u> I myself serve the law of God; but with the flesh the law of sin.

Romans 8.5 8 For they that are after the flesh do <u>mind</u> the things of the flesh; but they that are after the Spirit the things of the Spirit.

Romans 8.6 For to be carnally <u>minded</u> [is] death; but to be spiritually <u>minded</u> [is] life and peace.

8.7 Because the carnal <u>mind</u> [is] enmity against God: for it is not subject to the law of God, neither indeed can be.

8.8 So then they that are in the flesh cannot please God.

Romans 8.13 For if ye live after the flesh, ye shall die: but if ye through the Spirit do mortify the deeds of the body, ye shall live.

Romans 12.2 And be not conformed to this world: but be ye transformed by the renewing of your mind, that ye may prove what [is] that good, and acceptable, and perfect, will of God.

1 Corinthians 2.16 For who hath known the mind of the Lord, that he may instruct him? But we have the mind of Christ.

Ephesians 2.3 Among whom also we all had our conversation in times past in the lusts of our flesh, fulfilling the desires of the flesh and of the mind; and were by nature the children of wrath, even as others.

Ephesians 4.23-24,27 And be renewed in the spirit of your mind;

4.24 And that ye put on the new man, which after God is created in righteousness and true holiness.

4.27 Neither give place to the devil.

2 Timothy 1.7 For God hath not given us the spirit of fear; but of power, and of love, and of a sound mind.

Titus 1.15-16 Unto the pure all things [are] pure: but unto them that are defiled and unbelieving [is] nothing pure; but even their mind and conscience is defiled.

16 They profess that they know God; but in works they deny [him], being abominable, and disobedient, and unto every good work reprobate.

1 Peter 1.13 Wherefore gird up the loins of your mind, be sober, and hope to the end for the grace that is to be brought unto you at the revelation of Jesus Christ;

James 1.8 A double minded man [is] unstable in all his ways. (Double minded means two souls.)

James 4.7 Submit yourselves therefore to God. Resist the devil, and he will flee from you.

James 4.8 Draw nigh to God, and he will draw nigh to you. Cleanse [your] hands, [ye] sinners; and purify [your] hearts, [ye] double minded.

1 Chronicles 16.15 Be ye mindful always of his covenant; the word [which] he commanded to a thousand generations;

2 Corinthians 3.14 But their minds were blinded: for until this day remaineth the same vail untaken away in the reading of the old testament; which [vail] is done away in Christ.

2 Corinthians 4.4 In whom the god of this world hath blinded the minds of them which believe not, lest the light of the glorious gospel of Christ, who is the image of God, should shine unto them.

2 Corinthians 11.3 But I fear, lest by any means, as the serpent beguiled Eve through his subtilty, so your minds should be corrupted from the simplicity that is in Christ.

Philippians 4.7 And the peace of God, which passeth all understanding, shall keep your hearts and minds through Christ Jesus.

Philippians 4.8 Finally, brethren, whatsoever things are true, whatsoever things [are] honest, whatsoever things [are] just, whatsoever things [are] pure, whatsoever things [are] lovely, whatsoever things [are] of good report; if [there be] any virtue, and if [there be] any praise, think on these things.

Philippians 4.13 I can do all things through Christ which strengtheneth me.

Philippians 4.19 But my God shall supply all your need according to his riches in glory by Christ Jesus.

CHAPTER 30

STABLE IN ALL YOUR WAYS

James 1:5 If any of you lack wisdom, let him ask of God, that giveth to all men liberally, and upbraideth not; and it shall be given him.
James 1:6 But let him ask in faith, nothing wavering. For he that wavereth is like a wave of the sea driven with the wind and tossed.
James 1:7 For let not that man think that he shall receive any thing of the Lord.
James 1:8 A double minded man is UNSTABLE IN ALL HIS WAYS.

Let's take the word 'sin' off the table and all its negative ramifications and not consider it for now. Instead, let's use the words lust or desire.

If you are unstable in any part of your life, it may be because you are double-minded per James chapter one. Why is this? Because we have at least two minds, because we have a mind to serve lust or mammon, and another mind to serve God, another to serve sports or whatever.

Jesus said "no man can serve two masters. He'll either hate the one and love the other, hold on to one and despise the other. You cannot serve God and mammon at the same time." Matthew 6:24. You are loving lust and hating God, you are holding onto lusts and despising God. Jesus said in John 14:21, if you really love me you will obey and keep my words and I will come and manifest myself to you. So if we do not keep and obey his word, we hate Jesus. We have become hypocrites or mask wearers. We put on the Christian mask for church purposes, then upon leaving church we put on our normal mask that others don't know about.

But we usually have more than two masters that we serve in our social and business lives. There are so many things we can lust after because there are so many areas of input into our senses: watching all the cable TV shows we have recorded on DVR, internet videos, and all the other avenues of distraction and entertainment in our lives. The ungodly, worldly images we allow into our eye gates and the words and music we allow into our ear gates are infesting and cluttering our souls with junk. We are commanded to be unspotted by the world. Oops, too late!

Because we ARE serving God by doing godly things, but at the same time we are secretly indulging in satisfying our lust, we prove that we have at least two minds.

When you are addicted to lust of any kind – lust for sex, power, money, viewing nudity, consuming alcohol, drugs – you are sowing to the flesh, and will reap corruption as it states in Galatians 6.

What should we do? Set our affections on God and things of God: pray at least one hour a day, fast, give of yourself, consume the divine bread of life, drink of His Living Water, become strong in His Word.

Fasting from food for at least three or four days at a time on a consistent basis will help overcome lust and bring you closer to God. When you fast in secret you will be rewarded openly.

By focusing on Him and denying every area of your desires, you are proving to be single minded, and in time you will become stable in 100% of your ways.

Are you unstable physically? Are your limbs weak and wobbly?
Are you unstable financially? Has the money you need slowed down or stopped?

Is there instability in your marital life, or in the lives of your children and grandchildren?

Get single minded and 100% laser focused on the things of God and you will be solid and stable in 100% of the areas of your life.

CHAPTER 31

SCRIPTURES CONCERNING YOUR CHILDREN

Psalms 127:3 Lo, children are an heritage of the LORD: and the fruit of the womb is his reward.

Psalms 127:4 As arrows are in the hand of a mighty man; so are children of the youth.

Psalms 128:3 Thy wife shall be as a fruitful vine by the sides of thine house: thy children like olive plants round about thy table.

Psalms 128:6 Yea, thou shalt see thy children's children, and peace upon Israel.

Psalms 132:12 If thy children will keep my covenant and my testimony that I shall teach them, their children shall also sit upon thy throne for evermore.

Isaiah 8:18 Behold, I and the children whom the LORD hath given me are for signs and for wonders in Israel from the LORD of hosts, which dwelleth in mount Zion.

Isaiah 49:25 But thus saith the LORD, Even the captives of the mighty shall be taken away, and the prey of the terrible shall be delivered: for I will contend with him that contendeth with thee, and I will save thy children.

Isaiah 54:13 And all thy children shall be taught of the LORD; and great shall be the peace of thy children.

Psalms 112:2 His seed shall be mighty upon earth: the generation of the upright shall be blessed.

Proverbs 11:21 Though hand join in hand, the wicked shall not be unpunished: but the seed of the righteous shall be delivered.

Isaiah 44:3 For I will pour water upon him that is thirsty, and floods upon the dry ground: I will pour my spirit upon thy seed, and my blessing upon thine offspring:

Isaiah 59:21 As for me, this is my covenant with them, saith the LORD; My spirit that is upon thee, and my words which I have put in thy mouth, shall not depart out of thy mouth, nor out of the mouth of thy seed, nor out of the mouth of thy seed's seed, saith the LORD, from henceforth and for ever.

Isaiah 61:9 And their seed shall be known among the Gentiles, and their offspring among the people: all that see them shall acknowledge them, that they are the seed which the LORD hath blessed.

CHAPTER 32

DELIVERANCE AUTHORITY

These scriptures will build your faith in the Word of God concerning your authority as a Christian believer in Jesus Christ over Satan and his demons.

Matthew 28:18 And Jesus came and spake unto them, saying, All power is given unto me in heaven and in earth.

Luke 10:19 Behold, I give unto you power to tread on serpents and scorpions, and over all the power of the enemy: and nothing shall by any means hurt you.

Psalms 91:13 Thou shalt tread upon the lion and adder: the young lion and the dragon shalt thou trample under feet. (Lion, adder, and dragon are symbolic of demon spirits.)

1 John 3:8 He that commits sin is of the devil; for the devil sins from the beginning. For this purpose the Son of God was manifested, that he might destroy the works of the devil.

Hebrews 2:14 Forasmuch then as the children are partakers of flesh and blood, he also himself likewise took part of the same (flesh and blood); that through death he might destroy him that had the power of death, that is, the devil;

Hebrews 2:15 And deliver them who through fear of death were all their lifetime subject to bondage.

Colossians 1:13 Who hath delivered us from the power of darkness, and hath translated [us] into the kingdom of his dear Son:

Colossians 2:15 [And] having spoiled principalities and powers, he made a show of them openly, triumphing over them in it.

Acts 10:38 How God anointed Jesus of Nazareth with the Holy Ghost and with power: who went about doing good and healing all that were oppressed of the devil; for God was with him.

Isaiah 54:17 No weapon that is formed against thee shall prosper; and every tongue [that] shall rise against thee in judgment thou shalt condemn. This [is] the heritage of the servants of the LORD, and their righteousness is of me, saith the LORD.

John 14:12 Verily, verily, I say unto you, He that believeth on me, the works that I do shall he do also; and greater [works] than these shall he do; because I go unto my Father.

Mark 16:17 And these signs shall follow them that believe; In my name shall they cast out devils; they shall speak with new tongues;

Mark 16:18 They shall take up serpents; and if they drink any deadly thing, it shall not hurt them; they shall lay hands on the sick, and they shall recover.

Acts 16:18 And this did she many days. But Paul, being grieved, turned and said to the spirit, I command thee in the name of Jesus Christ to come out of her. And he came out the same hour.

Luke 10:17 And the seventy returned again with joy, saying, Lord, even the devils are subject unto us through thy name.

Luke 9:1 Then he called his twelve disciples together, and gave them power and authority over all devils, and to cure diseases.

Matthew 10:8 Heal the sick, cleanse the lepers, raise the dead, cast out devils: freely ye have received, freely give.

Colossians 2:9 For in him dwelleth all the fullness of the Godhead bodily.
Colossians 2:10 And ye are complete in him, which is the head of all principality and power:

Ephesians 2:5 Even when we were dead in sins, hath quickened us together with Christ, (by grace ye are saved;)
Ephesians 2:6 And hath raised us up together, and made us sit together in heavenly places in Christ Jesus:

Romans 8:11 But if the Spirit of him that raised up Jesus from the dead dwell in you, he that raised up Christ from the dead shall also quicken (enliven) your mortal bodies by his Spirit that dwelleth in you.

Ephesians 1:21-23 Far above all principality, and power, and might, and dominion, and every name that is named, not only in this world, but also in that which is to come:
22 And hath put all things under his feet, and gave him to be the head over all things to the church,
23 Which is his body, the fullness of him that filleth all in all.

1 John 4:4 Ye are of God, little children, and have overcome them: because greater is he that is in you, than he that is in the world.

1 John 4:17 Herein is our love made perfect, that we may have boldness in the day of judgment: because as he is, so are we in this world.

Hebrews 1:13 But to which of the angels said he at any time, Sit on my right hand, until I make thine enemies thy footstool?

Hebrews 10:12 But this man, after he had offered one sacrifice for sins for ever, sat down on the right hand of God;
Hebrews 10:13 From henceforth expecting till his enemies be made his footstool.

Romans 8:37 Nay, in all these things we are more than conquerors through him that loved us.

2 Timothy 1:7 For God hath not given us the spirit of fear; but of power, and of love, and of a sound mind.

Isaiah 41:10 Fear thou not; for I am with thee: be not dismayed; for I am thy God: I will strengthen thee; yea, I will help thee; yea, I will uphold thee with the right hand of my righteousness.

Luke 11:20 But if I with the finger of God cast out devils, no doubt the kingdom of God is come upon you.
Luke 11:21 When a strong man armed keepeth his palace, his goods are in peace:
Luke 11:22 But when a stronger than he shall come upon him, and overcome him, he taketh from him all his armour wherein he trusted, and divideth his spoils.

Matthew 18:18 Verily I say unto you, Whatsoever ye shall bind on earth shall be bound in heaven: and whatsoever ye shall loose on earth shall be loosed in heaven.

The Power of the Blood of Jesus

Revelations 12:11 And they overcame him by the blood of the Lamb, and by the word of their testimony; and they loved not their lives unto the death.

Leviticus 17:11 For the life of the flesh is in the blood: and I have given it to you upon the altar to make an atonement for your souls: for it is the blood that maketh an atonement for the soul.

Leviticus 17:14 For it is the life of all flesh; the blood of it is for the life thereof: therefore I said unto the children of Israel, Ye shall eat the blood of no manner of flesh: for the life of all flesh is the blood thereof: whosoever eateth it shall be cut off.

1 Peter 1:18 Forasmuch as ye know that ye were not redeemed with corruptible things, as silver and gold, from your vain conversation received by tradition from your fathers;
1 Peter 1:19 But with the precious blood of Christ, as of a lamb without blemish and without spot:

2 Kings 6:16 And he answered, Fear not: for they that be with us are more than they that be with them.

Ephesians 1:7 In whom we have redemption through his blood, the forgiveness of sins, according to the riches of his grace;

Colossians 1:14 In whom we have redemption through his blood, [even] the forgiveness of sins:

Revelations 5:9 And they sung a new song, saying, Thou art worthy to take the book, and to open the seals thereof: for thou wast slain, and hast redeemed us to God by thy blood out of every kindred, and tongue, and people, and nation;

Hebrews 12:24 And to Jesus the mediator of the new covenant, and to the blood of sprinkling, that speaketh better things than that of Abel.

1 Peter 1:2 Elect according to the foreknowledge of God the Father, through sanctification of the Spirit, unto obedience and sprinkling of the blood of Jesus Christ: Grace unto you, and peace, be multiplied.

Hebrews 10:19 Having therefore, brethren, boldness to enter into the holiest by the blood of Jesus,
Hebrews 10:22 Let us draw near with a true heart in full assurance of faith, having our hearts sprinkled from an evil conscience, and our bodies washed with pure water.

Hebrews 9:12 Neither by the blood of goats and calves, but by his own blood he entered in once into the holy place, having obtained eternal redemption for us.
Hebrews 9:13 For if the blood of bulls and of goats, and the ashes of an heifer sprinkling the unclean, sanctifieth to the purifying of the flesh:
Hebrews 9:14 How much more shall the blood of Christ, who through the eternal Spirit offered himself without spot to God, purge your conscience from dead works to serve the living God?

Romans 3:24 Being justified freely by his grace through the redemption that is in Christ Jesus:
Romans 3:25 Whom God hath set forth to be a propitiation through faith in his blood, to declare his righteousness for the remission of sins that are past, through the forbearance of God;

1 John 1:7 But if we walk in the light, as he is in the light, we have fellowship one with another, and the blood of Jesus Christ his Son cleanseth us from all sin.

Hebrews 13:12 Wherefore Jesus also, that he might sanctify the people with his own blood, suffered without (outside) the gate.

Ephesians 2:13 But now in Christ Jesus ye who sometimes were far off are made nigh (brought near) by the blood of Christ.

1 John 5:8 And there are three that bear witness in earth, the Spirit, and the water, and the blood: and these three agree in one.

The Light

Psalms 119:105 Thy word [is] a lamp unto my feet, and a light unto my path.
Psalms 119:130 The entrance of thy words giveth light; it giveth understanding unto the simple.

Isaiah 58:8 Then shall thy light break forth as the morning, and thine health shall spring forth speedily: and thy righteousness shall go before thee; the glory of the LORD shall be thy rereward (rear guard of an army).

Ephesians 1:18 The eyes of your understanding being enlightened; that ye may know what is the hope of his calling, and what the riches of the glory of his inheritance in the saints,

Overcoming Fear

Deuteronomy 28:7 The LORD shall cause thine enemies that rise up against thee to be smitten before thy face: they shall come out against thee one way, and flee before thee seven ways.

Deuteronomy 31:8 And the LORD, he it is that doth go before thee; he will be with thee, he will not fail thee, neither forsake thee: fear not, neither be dismayed.

Psalms 23:1 The LORD is my shepherd; I shall not want.
Psalms 23:4 Yea, though I walk through the valley of the shadow of death, I will fear no evil: for thou art with me; thy rod and thy staff they comfort me.

Joshua 1:5 There shall not any man be able to stand before thee all the days of thy life: as I was with Moses, so I will be with thee: I will not fail thee, nor forsake thee.
Joshua 1:9 Have not I commanded thee? Be strong and of a good courage; be not afraid, neither be thou dismayed: for the LORD thy God is with thee whithersoever thou goest.

Psalms 91:5 Thou shalt not be afraid for the terror by night; nor for the arrow that flieth by day;
Psalms 91:6 Nor for the pestilence that walketh in darkness; nor for the destruction that wasteth at noonday.
Psalms 91:7 A thousand shall fall at thy side, and ten thousand at thy right hand; but it shall not come nigh thee.
Psalms 91:8 Only with thine eyes shalt thou behold and see the reward of the wicked.

Psalms 27:1 The LORD is my light and my salvation; whom shall I fear? the LORD is the strength of my life; of whom shall I be afraid?
Psalms 27:3 Though a host should encamp against me, my heart shall not fear: though war should rise against me, in this will I be confident.
Psalms 46:1 God is our refuge and strength, a very present help in trouble.
Psalms 46:2 Therefore will not we fear, though the earth be removed, and though the mountains be carried into the midst of the sea;

Isaiah 41:10 Fear thou not; for I am with thee: be not dismayed; for I am thy God: I will strengthen thee; yea, I will help thee; yea, I will uphold thee with the right hand of my righteousness.

Isaiah 43:1 But now thus saith the LORD that created thee, O Jacob, and he that formed thee, O Israel, Fear not: for I have redeemed thee, I have called thee by thy name; thou art mine.
Isaiah 43:2 When thou passest through the waters, I will be with thee; and through the rivers, they shall not overflow thee: when thou walkest through the fire, thou shalt not be burned; neither shall the flame kindle upon thee.
Isaiah 43:3 For I am the LORD thy God, the Holy One of Israel, thy Saviour: I gave Egypt for thy ransom, Ethiopia and Seba for thee.

1 John 4:17 Herein is our love made perfect, that we may have boldness in the day of judgment: because as he is, so are we in this world.
1 John 4:18 There is no fear in love; but perfect love casteth out fear: because fear hath torment. He that feareth is not made perfect in love.

Psalms 149:6 Let the high praises of God be in their mouth, and a two-edged sword in their hand;
Psalms 149:8 To bind their kings with chains, and their nobles with fetters of iron;

Psalms 8:2 Out of the mouth of babes and sucklings hast thou ordained strength because of thine enemies, that thou mightest still the enemy and the avenger.

Luke 4:18 The Spirit of the Lord is upon me, because he hath anointed me to preach the gospel to the poor; he hath sent me to heal the brokenhearted, to preach deliverance to the captives, and recovering of sight to the blind, to set at liberty them that are bruised,
Luke 4:19 To preach the acceptable year of the Lord.

Isaiah 49:24 Shall the prey be taken from the mighty, or the lawful captive delivered?
Isaiah 49:25 But thus saith the LORD, Even the captives of the mighty shall be taken away, and the prey of the terrible shall be delivered: for I will contend with him that contendeth with thee, and I will save thy children.

2 Corinthians 10:4 For the weapons of our warfare are not carnal, but mighty through God to the pulling down of strong holds;
2 Corinthians 10:5 Casting down imaginations, and every high thing that exalteth itself against the knowledge of God, and bringing into captivity every thought to the obedience of Christ;

Matthew 12:28 But if I cast out devils by the Spirit of God, then the kingdom of God is come unto you.
Matthew 12:29 Or else how can one enter into a strong man's house, and spoil his goods, except he first bind the strong man? and then he will spoil his house.

Matthew 16:18 And I say also unto thee, That thou art Peter, and upon this rock I will build my church; and the gates of hell shall not prevail against it.
Matthew 16:19 And I will give unto thee the keys of the kingdom of heaven: and whatsoever thou shalt bind on earth shall be bound in heaven: and whatsoever thou shalt loose on earth shall be loosed in heaven.

1 John 4:1 Beloved, believe not every spirit, but try the spirits whether they are of God: because many false prophets are gone out into the world.
1 John 4:2 Hereby know ye the Spirit of God: Every spirit that confesseth that Jesus Christ is come in the flesh is of God:
1 John 4:3 And every spirit that confesseth not that Jesus Christ is come in the flesh is not of God: and this is that spirit of antichrist, whereof ye have heard that it should come; and even now already is it in the world.
1 John 4:4 Ye are of God, little children, and have overcome them: because greater is he that is in you, than he that is in the world.
1 John 4:5 They are of the world: therefore speak they of the world, and the world heareth them.

Romans 8:37 Nay, in all these things we are more than conquerors through him that loved us.

Ephesians 2:6 And hath raised us up together, and made us sit together in heavenly places in Christ Jesus:
Ephesians 1:21 Far above all principality, and power, and might, and dominion, and every name that is named, not only in this world, but also in that which is to come:

2 Timothy 1:7 For God hath not given us the spirit of fear; but of power, and of love, and of a sound mind.

CHAPTER 33

HOW TO PRAY FOR THE LOST, OR THOSE WHO HAVE GONE ASTRAY

Saul the religious terrorist had an encounter with God in Acts chapter 9.

He was prayed for in Acts 9.18 and "scales fell from his eyes." Why did that happen?

Job 41.15-16 speaks of Leviathan:
15 [His] scales [are his] pride, shut up together [as with] a close seal.
16 One is so near to another, that no air can come between them.

Leviathan is portrayed here as a sea monster, that twisting serpent –
This passage is speaking of a demon spirit that causes spiritual blindness, and twisting of the Word of God.

When he was prayed for, Saul was delivered supernaturally from the Leviathan spirit, and he could see clearly in the physical realm as well as the spiritual realm.

2 Corinthians 4.4 … the god of this world (age) hath blinded the minds (noema) of them which believe not, lest the light of the glorious gospel of Christ, who is the image of God, should shine unto them.

2 Corinthians 10: 3 For though we walk in the flesh, we do not war after the flesh:

(Expanded) 3 - For though we make our way and progress through this life in our flesh and blood body, we do not plan, strategize and undertake a military expedition using our carnal ways and means.

4 For the weapons of our warfare are not carnal, but mighty through God to the pulling down of strong holds;

(Expanded) 4 - For our military warfare weapons are not carnal or fleshly, but rather, like a large box of plastic explosives or dynamite, able and powerful enough to completely demolish and destroy the fortress of that person's arguments and reasonings by which they dispute and endeavor to fortify their opinion and defend it against his opponent, which is God and the things of God, (like salvation, living holy, etc.)

5 Casting down imaginations and every high thing that exalts itself against the knowledge of God, and bringing into captivity every thought (noema) to the obedience of Christ;

(Expanded) 5 – Through the Spirit of God we will detonate our spiritual explosives, thereby demolishing their reasonings, belief systems, mindsets which are hostile against God's plan for their life, and every great wall of pride they have lifted up as a barrier against the knowledge of God and God's workings in their life, and placing their antagonistic, evil reasonings, schemes, plans, & devices under arrest and have them brought under control to the obedience, compliance, and submission of Jesus Christ.

Pray this:

"According to 2 Corinthians 10:3, 4 & 5, God's WORD tells me that I have weapons powerful enough to defeat the enemy. I have faith to believe God will empower these weapons with His miracle working power to demolish this part of the stronghold in ____ life. So in the name of Jesus Christ, I command the mindsets, reasonings and belief systems that are holding them captive to be torn down in their mind, to free them to see the Gospel clearly. I demolish you stronghold of ___." (Or whatever it is that is controlling them.)

"In the name of Jesus I destroy the stronghold of pride in _____, and I say they will bow their knees to God; I take authority and dominion over you and I loose them from this root of pride. In Jesus name I demolish it."

"I now, by the weapons that God has given to me, and by the power of the Holy Spirit being released, I take authority over every thought you try to send to them, every reason, every excuse and every strategy and plan that you have to keep _____ blinded to the truth, I say NO to it. I demolish it now in Jesus name. I capture that now, I place you under arrest and I say it will not work against them any more. I will be their shield, and by faith I stand between them and you, and I say you will not work this successfully against them in Jesus name."

We're going to capture and demolish the thoughts, plans and schemes of the enemy and we're going to release _____ to hear and understand what God is really saying and obey God.

In Jesus name, Amen!"

CHAPTER 34

PREACHING THE GOSPEL

Here is a word study related to witnessing and preaching the Good News, the Gospel of Jesus Christ. It is meant to encourage you and show you examples of what Jesus has done, what God wants you to do, and what others have done. Get these scriptures in your heart and arm yourself with God's Word before you go into enemy territory for battle, to snatch souls from the grip of evil.

Mark 3:13-15 And he goeth up into a mountain, and calleth unto him whom he would: and they came unto him.
14 And he ordained twelve, that they should be with him, and that he might send them forth to preach,
15 And to have power to heal sicknesses, and to cast out devils:

Luke 4:18 The Spirit of the Lord is upon me, because he hath anointed me to preach the gospel to the poor; he hath sent me to heal the brokenhearted, to preach deliverance to the captives, and recovering of sight to the blind, to set at liberty them that are bruised,
19 To preach the acceptable year of the Lord.

Luke 9:1 Then he called his twelve disciples together, and gave them power and authority over all devils, and to cure diseases.
9:2 And he sent them to preach the kingdom of God, and to heal the sick.
9:6 And they departed, and went through the towns, preaching the gospel, and healing every where.

Acts 17:3 Opening and alleging, that Christ must needs have suffered, and risen again from the dead; and that this Jesus, whom I preach unto you, is Christ.

Romans 10:8 But what saith it? The word is nigh thee, [even] in thy mouth, and in thy heart: that is, the word of faith, which we preach;

Matthew 9:37 Then saith he unto his disciples, The harvest truly [is] plenteous, but the labourers [are] few;
9:38 Pray ye therefore the Lord of the harvest, that he will send forth labourers into his harvest.

1 Corinthians 1:17-31 For Christ sent me not to baptize, but to preach the gospel: not with wisdom of words, lest the cross of Christ should be made of none effect.
1:18 For the preaching of the cross is to them that perish foolishness; but unto us which are saved it is the power of God.

1:19 For it is written, I will destroy the wisdom of the wise, and will bring to nothing the understanding of the prudent.
1:20 Where [is] the wise? where [is] the scribe? where [is] the disputer of this world? hath not God made foolish the wisdom of this world?
1:21 For after that in the wisdom of God the world by wisdom knew not God, it pleased God by the foolishness of preaching to save them that believe.
1:22 For the Jews require a sign, and the Greeks seek after wisdom:
1:23 But we preach Christ crucified, unto the Jews a stumblingblock, and unto the Greeks foolishness;
1:24 But unto them which are called, both Jews and Greeks, Christ the power of God, and the wisdom of God.
1:25 Because the foolishness of God is wiser than men; and the weakness of God is stronger than men.
1:26 For ye see your calling, brethren, how that not many wise men after the flesh, not many mighty, not many noble, [are called]:
1:27 But God hath chosen the foolish things of the world to confound the wise; and God hath chosen the weak things of the world to confound the things which are mighty;
1:28 And base things of the world, and things which are despised, hath God chosen, [yea], and things which are not, to bring to nought things that are:
1:29 That no flesh should glory in his presence.
1:30 But of him are ye in Christ Jesus, who of God is made unto us wisdom, and righteousness, and sanctification, and redemption:
1:31 That, according as it is written, He that glorieth, let him glory in the Lord.

1 Corinthians 2:1-5 And I, brethren, when I came to you, came not with excellency of speech or of wisdom, declaring unto you the testimony of God.
2:2 For I determined not to know any thing among you, save Jesus Christ, and him crucified.
2:3 And I was with you in weakness, and in fear, and in much trembling.
2:4 And my speech and my preaching was not with enticing words of man's wisdom, but in demonstration of the Spirit and of power:
2:5 That your faith should not stand in the wisdom of men, but in the power of God.

1 Corinthians 9:14 Even so hath the Lord ordained that they which preach the gospel should live of the gospel.

Ephesians 3:8 Unto me, who am less than the least of all saints, is this grace given, that I should preach among the Gentiles the unsearchable riches of Christ;

2 Timothy 4:2 Preach the word; be instant in season, out of season; reprove, rebuke, exhort with all longsuffering and doctrine.

Mark 6:12 And they went out and preached that men should repent.
6:13 And they cast out many devils, and anointed with oil many that were sick, and healed [them].

Mark 16:15-20 And he said unto them, Go ye into all the world, and preach the gospel to every creature.
16 He that believeth and is baptized shall be saved; but he that believeth not shall be damned.
20 And they went forth, and preached everywhere, the Lord working with them, and confirming the word with signs following. Amen.

Luke 24:25 Then he said unto them, O fools, and slow of heart to believe all that the prophets have spoken:
24:26 Ought not Christ to have suffered these things, and to enter into his glory?
24:27 And beginning at Moses and all the prophets, he expounded unto them in all the scriptures the things concerning himself.
24:32 And they said one to another, Did not our heart burn within us, while he talked with us by the way, and while he opened to us the scriptures?
24:44 And he said unto them, These [are] the words which I spake unto you, while I was yet with you, that all things must be fulfilled, which were written in the law of Moses, and [in] the prophets, and [in] the psalms, concerning me.
24:45 Then opened he their understanding, that they might understand the scriptures,
24:46 And said unto them, Thus it is written, and thus it behooved Christ to suffer, and to rise from the dead the third day:
24:47 And that repentance and remission of sins should be preached in his name among all nations, beginning at Jerusalem.
24:48 And ye are witnesses of these things.

Acts 4:2 Being grieved that they taught the people, and preached through Jesus the resurrection from the dead.

Acts 9:20 And straightway Paul preached Christ in the synagogues, that he is the Son of God.
Acts 9:27 But Barnabas took him, and brought [him] to the apostles, and declared unto them how he had seen the Lord in the way, and that he had spoken to him, and how he had preached boldly at Damascus in the name of Jesus.

Acts 13:38 Be it known unto you therefore, men [and] brethren, that through this man is preached unto you the forgiveness of sins:
13:39 And by him all that believe are justified from all things, from which ye could not be justified by the law of Moses.

1 Peter 1:12 Unto whom it was revealed, that not unto themselves, but unto us they did minister the things, which are now reported unto you by them that have preached the gospel unto you with the Holy Ghost sent down from heaven; which things the angels desire to look into.

Light

Matthew 4:16 The people which sat in darkness saw great light; and to them which sat in the region and shadow of death light is sprung up.

John 1:4 In him was life; and the life was the light of men.

John 3:19 And this is the condemnation, that light is come into the world, and men loved darkness rather than light, because their deeds were evil.

John 1:1 In the beginning was the Word, and the Word was with God, and the Word was God.
Psalms 119:105 Thy word [is] a lamp unto my feet, and a light unto my path.
119:130 The entrance of thy words giveth light; it giveth understanding unto the simple.
Matthew 5:14 Ye are the light of the world. A city that is set on an hill cannot be hid.
5:16 Let your light so shine before men, that they may see your good works, and glorify your Father which is in heaven.

Philemon 2:15 That ye may be blameless and harmless, the sons of God, without rebuke, in the midst of a crooked and perverse nation, among whom ye shine as lights in the world;

Acts 13:47 For so hath the Lord commanded us, [saying], I have set thee to be a light of the Gentiles, that thou shouldest be for salvation unto the ends of the earth.
Acts 17:6 And when they found them not, they drew Jason and certain brethren unto the rulers of the city, crying, These that have turned the world upside down are come hither also;

Acts 26:16 But rise, and stand upon thy feet: for I have appeared unto thee for this purpose, to make thee a minister and a witness both of these things which thou hast seen, and of those things in the which I will appear unto thee;
26:17 Delivering thee from the people, and [from] the Gentiles, unto whom now I send thee,
26:18 To open their eyes, [and] to turn [them] from darkness to light, and [from] the power of Satan unto God, that they may receive forgiveness of sins, and inheritance among them which are sanctified by faith that is in me.

Ezekiel 33:8 When I say unto the wicked, O wicked [man], thou shalt surely die; if thou dost not speak to warn the wicked from his way, that wicked [man] shall die in his iniquity; but his blood will I require at thine hand.
33:9 Nevertheless, if thou warn the wicked of his way to turn from it; if he do not turn from his way, he shall die in his iniquity; but thou hast delivered thy soul.

Romans 1:15 So, as much as in me is, I am ready to preach the gospel to you that are at Rome also.
1:16 For I am not ashamed of the gospel of Christ: for it is the power of God unto salvation to every one that believeth; to the Jew first, and also to the Greek.

Acts 26:22 Having therefore obtained help of God, I continue unto this day, witnessing both to small and great, saying none other things than those which the prophets and Moses did say should come:

26:23 That Christ should suffer, [and] that he should be the first that should rise from the dead, and should show light unto the people, and to the Gentiles.

Proverbs 29:25 The fear of man bringeth a snare: but whoso putteth his trust in the LORD shall be safe.

Proverbs 28:1 The wicked flee when no man pursueth: but the righteous are bold as a lion.

Acts 4:29 And now, Lord, behold their threatenings: and grant unto thy servants, that with all boldness they may speak thy word,
4:30 By stretching forth thine hand to heal; and that signs and wonders may be done by the name of thy holy child Jesus.

Hebrews 2:3 How shall we escape, if we neglect so great salvation; which at the first began to be spoken by the Lord, and was confirmed unto us by them that heard [him];
2:4 God also bearing [them] witness, both with signs and wonders, and with divers miracles, and gifts of the Holy Ghost, according to his own will?

Acts 6:4 But we will give ourselves continually to prayer, and to the ministry of the word.
6:5 And the saying pleased the whole multitude: and they chose Stephen, a man full of faith and of the Holy Ghost, and Philip, and Prochorus, and Nicanor, and Timon, and Parmenas, and Nicolas a proselyte of Antioch:
6:8 And Stephen, full of faith and power, did great wonders and miracles among the people.
6:9 Then there arose certain of the synagogue, which is called [the synagogue] of the Libertines, and Cyrenians, and Alexandrians, and of them of Cilicia and of Asia, disputing with Stephen.
6:10 And they were not able to resist the wisdom and the spirit by which he spake.

Matthew 18:18 Verily I say unto you, Whatsoever ye shall bind on earth shall be bound in heaven: and whatsoever ye shall loose on earth shall be loosed in heaven.

Acts 1:8 But ye shall receive power, after that the Holy Ghost is come upon you: and ye shall be witnesses unto me both in Jerusalem, and in all Judaea, and in Samaria, and unto the uttermost part of the earth. "I have received POWER since the Holy Ghost has come upon me. Power to witness and preach."

Luke 24:49 And, behold, I send the promise of my Father upon you: but tarry ye in the city of Jerusalem, until ye be endued with power from on high. **(I have been endued with POWER from on high!)**

Isaiah 59:19 So shall they fear the name of the LORD from the west, and his glory from the rising of the sun. When the enemy shall come in like a flood, the Spirit of the LORD shall lift up a standard against him.

Acts 3:16 And his name through faith in his name hath made this man strong, whom ye see and know: yea, the faith which is by him hath given him this perfect soundness in the presence of you all.

Jesus commanded us to raise the dead

Hebrews 13:8 Jesus Christ the same yesterday, and today, and for ever.
    ... I am the resurrection and the life.
    ... heal the sick, raise the dead.
    ... Jesus destroyed him that HAD the power of death.
    ... The law of the Spirit of life in Christ Jesus has made us free from the law of sin and death.

Matthew 15:30 And great multitudes came unto him, having with them [those that were] lame, blind, dumb, maimed, and many others, and cast them down at Jesus' feet; and he healed them:
15:31 Insomuch that the multitude wondered, when they saw the dumb to speak, the maimed to be whole, the lame to walk, and the blind to see: and they glorified the God of Israel.

Acts 8:4 Therefore they that were scattered abroad went every where preaching the word.
8:5 Then Philip went down to the city of Samaria, and preached Christ unto them.
8:6 And the people with one accord gave heed unto those things which Philip spake, hearing and seeing the miracles which he did.
8:7 For unclean spirits, crying with loud voice, came out of many that were possessed [with them]: and many taken with palsies, and that were lame, were healed.
8:8 And there was great joy in that city.
8:12 But when they believed Philip preaching the things concerning the kingdom of God, and the name of Jesus Christ, they were baptized, both men and women.

Daniel 12:2 And many of them that sleep in the dust of the earth shall awake, some to everlasting life, and some to shame [and] everlasting contempt.
12:3 And they that be wise shall shine as the brightness of the firmament; and they that turn many to righteousness as the stars for ever and ever.
Proverbs 11:30 The fruit of the righteous [is] a tree of life; and he that winneth souls [is] wise.

Luke 10:20 Notwithstanding in this rejoice not, that the spirits are subject unto you; but rather rejoice, because your names are written in heaven.

Overcoming the Fear of Man

    When you go witnessing, remember that you are speaking to them in the name of Jesus. When you speak in the name of someone, you are speaking in his behalf, representing him. Therefore, you are there in His stead. He couldn't be there in the flesh, but you are taking His place, saying and doing what He would do, if He were here. Anything someone says or does to you, consider it as them saying or doing it to Jesus

Himself. Remember Jesus, your Good Shepherd, is walking with you by your side, and you are filled with the Holy Ghost POWER OF GOD!

Proverbs 29:25 The fear of man bringeth a snare: but whoso putteth his trust in the LORD shall be safe.

John 15:16 Ye have not chosen me, but I have chosen you, and ordained you, that ye should go and bring forth fruit, and [that] your fruit should remain: that whatsoever ye shall ask of the Father in my name, he may give it you.

Psalms 2:8 Ask of me, and I shall give [thee] the heathen [for] thine inheritance, and the uttermost parts of the earth [for] thy possession.
John 15:17 These things I command you, that ye love one another.
15:18 If the world hate you, ye know that it hated me before [it hated] you.
15:19 If ye were of the world, the world would love his own: but because ye are not of the world, but I have chosen you out of the world, therefore the world hateth you.
15:20 Remember the word that I said unto you, The servant is not greater than his lord. If they have persecuted me, they will also persecute you; if they have kept my saying, they will keep yours also.
15:21 But all these things will they do unto you for my name's sake, because they know not him that sent me.
Matthew 10:25 It is enough for the disciple that he be as his master, and the servant as his lord. If they have called the master of the house Beelzebub, how much more [shall they call] them of his household?
10:26 Fear them not therefore: for there is nothing covered, that shall not be revealed; and hid, that shall not be known.
10:27 What I tell you in darkness, [that] speak ye in light: and what ye hear in the ear, [that] preach ye upon the housetops.
10:28 And fear not them which kill the body, but are not able to kill the soul: but rather fear him which is able to destroy both soul and body in hell.

Hebrews 13:5 [Let your] conversation [be] without covetousness; [and be] content with such things as ye have: for he hath said, I will never leave thee, nor forsake thee.
13:6 So that we may boldly say, The Lord [is] my helper, and I will not fear what man shall do unto me.

1 Peter 4:14 If ye be reproached for the name of Christ, happy [are ye]; for the spirit of glory and of God resteth upon you: on their part he is evil spoken of, but on your part he is glorified.
4:16 Yet if [any man suffer] as a Christian, let him not be ashamed; but let him glorify God on this behalf.

Luke 6:22 Blessed are ye, when men shall hate you, and when they shall separate you [from their company], and shall reproach [you], and cast out your name as evil, for the Son of man's sake.
6:23 Rejoice ye in that day, and leap for joy: for, behold, your reward [is] great in heaven: for in the like manner did their fathers unto the prophets.

Psalms 27:1 The LORD [is] my light and my salvation; whom shall I fear? the LORD [is] the strength of my life; of whom shall I be afraid?

Luke 9:26 For whosoever shall be ashamed of me and of my words, of him shall the Son of man be ashamed, when he shall come in his own glory, and [in his] Father's, and of the holy angels.

Luke 7:23 And blessed is [he], whosoever shall not be offended in me.

Isaiah 51:7 Hearken unto me, ye that know righteousness, the people in whose heart [is] my law; fear ye not the reproach of men, neither be ye afraid of their revilings.

Jeremiah 1:8 Be not afraid of their faces: for I [am] with thee to deliver thee, saith the LORD.

Jeremiah 1:17 Thou therefore gird up thy loins, and arise, and speak unto them all that I command thee: be not dismayed at their faces, lest I confound thee before them.

CHAPTER 35

SEEKING GOD

Matthew 7:7 Ask, and it shall be given you; <u>seek</u>, and you shall find; knock, and it shall be opened unto you.
8 For every one that asks, receives; and he that <u>seeks</u>, finds; and to him that knocks, it shall be opened.

Hebrews 11.6 But without faith it is impossible to please him: for he that cometh to God must believe that he is, and that he is a rewarder of them that diligently <u>seek</u> him.

Proverbs 8:17 I love them that love Me; and those that <u>seek</u> Me early shall find Me.

Jeremiah 29:12 Then shall you call upon Me, and I will hearken unto you.
13 And you shall <u>seek</u> Me, and find Me, when you shall <u>search</u> for Me with all your heart.
14 And I will be found of you, saith the Lord: and I will turn away your captivity.

Joel 2:12 Therefore also now, saith the Lord, turn ye even to Me with all your heart, and with fasting, and with weeping, and with mourning.

Psalms 91:15 He shall call upon Me, and I will answer him.

Isaiah 58:9 Then shalt thou call, and the Lord shall answer; thou shalt cry, and He shall say, "Here I am".

John 4:23 The true worshippers worship the Father in spirit and in truth: for the Father <u>seeketh</u> such to worship Him.

John 10 I am His sheep, Jesus is my Shepherd. I hear His voice, and He calls me by my name. I follow Jesus, for I know His voice, and a stranger I will not follow, for I don't know the voice of strangers.

Amos 3:7 Surely the Lord God will do nothing, unless he reveals His secret (counsel) unto His servants the prophets.

Jeremiah 32:17 Ah Lord God! Behold, thou hast made the heaven and the earth by thy great power and stretched out arm, and there is nothing too hard for thee.
Jeremiah 32:27 Behold, I am the Lord, the God of all flesh: is there any thing too hard for me?

Jeremiah 33:3 Call unto Me, and I will answer thee, and show thee great and mighty things, which thou knowest not.
33:6 Behold, I will bring it health and cure, and I will cure them, and will reveal unto them the abundance of peace and truth.
33:9b ...and they shall fear and tremble for all the goodness and for all the prosperity that I procure unto them.
2 Chronicles 7:14 If my people, which are called by my name, shall humble themselves and pray, and seek my face, and turn from their wicked ways; then will I hear from heaven, and will forgive their sin, and will heal their land.

Psalms 46:10 Be still and know that I am God.

James 4:8 Draw near to God and He will draw near to you. Cleanse your hands, you sinners; and purify your hearts, you double-minded.
Matthew 6:18b And thy Father which seeth in secret shall reward thee openly.

John 14:21 He that loves Me shall be loved of My Father, and I will love him, and will manifest myself to him.

Matthew 6:33 Seek ye first the kingdom of God and His righteousness, and all these things shall be added unto you.

Scriptures on Seeking God
Seek

Deuteronomy 4.29 But if from thence thou shalt seek the LORD thy God, thou shalt find [him], if thou seek him with all thy heart and with all thy soul.

1 Chronicles 16.10 Glory ye in his holy name: let the heart of them rejoice that seek the LORD.
11 Seek the LORD and his strength, seek his face continually.

1 Chronicles 22.19 Now set your heart and your soul to seek the LORD your God; arise therefore, and build ye the sanctuary of the LORD God, to bring the ark of the

covenant of the LORD, and the holy vessels of God, into the house that is to be built to the name of the LORD.

2 Chronicles 11.16 And after them out of all the tribes of Israel such as set their hearts to seek the LORD God of Israel came to Jerusalem, to sacrifice unto the LORD God of their fathers.

2 Chronicles 15.2 And he went out to meet Asa, and said unto him, Hear ye me, Asa, and all Judah and Benjamin; The LORD [is] with you, while ye be with him; and if ye seek him, he will be found of you; but if ye forsake him, he will forsake you.

2 Chronicles 15.12 And they entered into a covenant to seek the LORD God of their fathers with all their heart and with all their soul;
13 That whosoever would not seek the LORD God of Israel should be put to death, whether small or great, whether man or woman.

2 Chronicles 19.3 Nevertheless there are good things found in thee (Jehoshaphat), in that thou hast taken away the groves out of the land, and hast prepared thine heart to seek God.

2 Chronicles 20.3 And Jehoshaphat feared, and set himself to seek the LORD, and proclaimed a fast throughout all Judah.
4 And Judah gathered themselves together, to ask [help] of the LORD: even out of all the cities of Judah they came to seek the LORD.

2 Chronicles 31.21 And in every work that he (Hezekiah) began in the service of the house of God, and in the law, and in the commandments, to seek his God, he did [it] with all his heart, and prospered.

2 Chronicles 34.3 For in the eighth year of his reign, while he (Josiah) was yet young, he began to seek after the God of David his father: and in the twelfth year he began to purge Judah and Jerusalem from the high places, and the groves, and the carved images, and the molten images.

Ezra 8.22 For I was ashamed to require of the king a band of soldiers and horsemen to help us against the enemy in the way: because we had spoken unto the king, saying, The hand of our God [is] upon all them for good that seek him; but his power and his wrath [is] against all them that forsake him. 23 So we fasted and besought our God for this: and he was intreated of us.

Psalms 9.10 And they that know thy name will put their trust in thee: for thou, LORD, hast not forsaken them that seek thee.

Psalms 14.2 The LORD looked down from heaven upon the children of men, to see if there were any that did understand, [and] seek God.

Psalms 27.8 [When thou saidst], Seek ye my face; my heart said unto thee, Thy face, LORD, will I seek.

Psalms 34.10 The young lions do lack, and suffer hunger: but they that seek the LORD shall not want any good [thing].

Psalms 40.16 Let all those that seek thee rejoice and be glad in thee: let such as love thy salvation say continually, The LORD be magnified.

Psalms 53.2 God looked down from heaven upon the children of men, to see if there were [any] that did understand, that did seek God.

Psalms 63.1 [[A Psalm of David, when he was in the wilderness of Judah.]] O God, thou [art] my God; early will I seek thee: my soul thirsteth for thee, my flesh longeth for thee in a dry and thirsty land, where no water is;

Psalms 105.4 Seek the LORD, and his strength: seek his face evermore.
Proverbs 8.17 I love them that love me; and those that seek me early shall find me.

Proverbs 28.5 Evil men understand not judgment: but they that seek the LORD understand all [things].

Isaiah 26.9 With my soul have I desired thee in the night; yea, with my spirit within me will I seek thee early: for when thy judgments [are] in the earth, the inhabitants of the world will learn righteousness.

Isaiah 55.6 Seek ye the LORD while he may be found, call ye upon him while he is near:

Jeremiah 29.13 And ye shall seek me, and find [me], when ye shall search for me with all your heart.

Daniel 9.3 And I set my face unto the Lord God, to seek by prayer and supplications, with fasting, and sackcloth, and ashes:

Hosea 5.15 I will go [and] return to my place, till they acknowledge their offence, and seek my face: in their affliction they will seek me early.

Hosea 10.12 Sow to yourselves in righteousness, reap in mercy; break up your fallow ground: for [it is] time to seek the LORD, till he come and rain righteousness upon you.

Zephaniah 2.3 Seek ye the LORD, all ye meek of the earth, which have wrought his judgment; seek righteousness, seek meekness: it may be ye shall be hid in the day of the LORD'S anger.

Acts 17.27 That they should seek the Lord, if haply they might feel after him, and find him, though he be not far from every one of us:

Sought

Exodus 33.7 And Moses took the tabernacle, and pitched it without the camp, afar off from the camp, and called it the Tabernacle of the congregation. And it came to pass, [that] every one which <u>sought</u> the LORD went out unto the tabernacle of the congregation, which [was] without the camp.

2 Chronicles 14.7 Therefore he said unto Judah, Let us build these cities, and make about [them] walls, and towers, gates, and bars, [while] the land [is] yet before us; because we have <u>sought</u> the LORD our God, we have <u>sought</u> [him], and he hath given us rest on every side. So they built and prospered.

2 Chronicles 15.4 But when they in their trouble did turn unto the LORD God of Israel, and <u>sought</u> him, he was found of them.

2 Chronicles 15.15 And all Judah rejoiced at the oath: for they had sworn with all their heart, and <u>sought</u> him with their whole desire; and he was found of them: and the LORD gave them rest round about.

Psalms 34.4 I <u>sought</u> the LORD, and he heard me, and delivered me from all my fears.

Romans 10.20 But Esaias is very bold, and saith, I was found of them that <u>sought</u> me not; I was made manifest unto them that asked not after me.

To order copies of this book and our other books, see our website, www.CypressCovePublishing.com or call Toll Free (888) 606-3257, or buy from Barnes & Noble (BN.com) or Amazon.com

ABOUT THE AUTHOR

Neal Bertrand received Jesus and his Holy Spirit heavenly prayer language in 1972. He grew up in Opelousas, Louisiana but has been living nearby in Lafayette since 1975. He is the father of three grown children, with two grandsons.

He is an author and publisher. His publishing company is Cypress Cove Publishing. He has written nine books with 100,000 copies sold including cookbooks, puzzle and activity books, and a WWII pictorial of his father's 600 war photos he took. He is a licensed and ordained minister and enjoys teaching the Bible. His websites are CypressCovePublishing.com and DadsWarPhotos.com.

www.ingramcontent.com/pod-product-compliance
Lightning Source LLC
Chambersburg PA
CBHW081350080526
44588CB00016B/2444